THE KOGAN PAGE GUIDE TO

WORKING IN THE MEDIA

SECOND EDITION

**Edited by
Allan Shepherd**

First published as *The Kogan Page Guide to Careers in the Media*, 1989
This second edition published 1997

Apart from any fair dealing for the purposes of research or private study, or criticism or review, as permitted under the Copyright, Designs and Patents Act, 1988, this publication may only be reproduced, stored or transmitted, in any form or by any means, with the prior permission in writing of the publishers, or in the case of reprographic reproduction in accordance with the terms of licences issued by the Copyright Licensing Agency. Enquiries concerning reproduction outside those terms should be sent to the publishers at the undermentioned address:

Kogan Page Limited
120 Pentonville Road
London N1 9JN

© Kogan Page 1997

British Library Cataloguing in Publication Data

A CIP record for this book is available from the British Library.

ISBN 0 7494 2139 8

Typeset by Kogan Page Ltd
Printed and bound in Great Britain by Clays Ltd, St Ives plc

Contents

	Acknowledgements	iv
	Introduction	1
1.	Broadcasting	7
2.	Film and Video	24
3.	The Theatre and Performance Arts	38
4.	Arts Administration, Sponsorship and Agency Work	52
5.	Publishing and Printing	60
6.	Writing	74
7.	Journalism	82
8.	Marketing, Advertising and Public Relations	95
9.	Art and Design and Photography	107
10.	How to Get a Job in the Media	120
	Index	134

Acknowledgements

The source material for this book comes mostly from current Kogan Page titles. I have made use of the following: *Careers in Art and Design* by Linda Ball and Noel Chapman, *Careers in Film and Video* by Ricki Ostrov and Howard Hall, *Careers in Journalism* by Peter Medina and Allan Shepherd, *Careers in Marketing, Advertising and Public Relations* by Caroline Hird and Joanna Grigg, *Careers in Publishing and Bookselling* by June Lines, *Careers in Television and Radio* by Michael Selby, *Careers in the Theatre* by Jean Richardson, *How to Choose a Career* by Vivien Donald and *The A–Z of Careers and Jobs*.

I would also like to thank the following organisations for the information they provided: the British Film Institute, UCAS, the Royal Photographic Society, the National Council for the Training of Journalists and *Writing Magazine*.

A note of thanks to my commissioning editor, June Lines, for all her support and encouragement over the past two years, and to Nicola Stephens, June's successor.

I would especially like to take this opportunity to thank my sister Hazel for lending me her computer for three weeks, without which I would never have completed this book anywhere near on time, and my mum Lesley, for giving me her continuing love and support.

Introduction

The nature of the media industry is such that most sectors are reliant on the others in some way or another. Industry partnerships exist within all sectors and quite often between them. This relationship appears either in the form of a co-operative venture between companies hoping to benefit from each others' talents, experiences and cash, such as Channel Four and the British Film Institute, or as a result of activities that are mutually dependent, ie advertising needs broadcasting and publishing to fulfil its creative ambitions and broadcasters and publishers need adverts, and the revenue they bring, to keep working.

Some particular media companies will draw upon the skills of a wide range of media workers. The film and theatre industry, for example, provides work for performers, technicians, writers, beauticians, designers, craftspeople, dressmakers, marketing personnel, accountants, secretaries, and indirectly feeds newspaper journalists, magazine editors, book publishers and merchandise manufacturers with raw material for work.

Occasionally, a technological development or a change in working patterns can effect the whole industry to a greater or lesser extent. The use of advanced computer technology and the changing relationship between unions and employees are two obvious examples. There used to be a time when much of the entertainment industry was a closed shop to those without a work 'ticket' from the largest entertainment union, BECTU (Broadcasting Entertainment Cinematograph and Theatre Union), but this is no longer the case.

Practices which once dominated the way the media industries operated have been replaced by other techniques. Media professionals continually find themselves in the awkward position of having to learn the new rules and work according to them. Someone who can stay ahead of the game will do well. Those who fall behind the times find themselves deprived of work or having to pursue other avenues. The media industry is highly competitive. Most job advertisements should carry the words: 'only ambitious people need apply'.

If you are 16 the chances are you will not remember the Wapping trades union dispute which signified the end of the print unions' dominance of the newspaper industry. Rupert Murdoch wanted to move the production offices of the *Sun* away from its traditional home in Fleet Street and into a technologically advanced warehouse outside the centre of London, in Wapping. Almost literally overnight, he computerised newspaper reporting, editing and printing so that copy could be fed through a computer, cut, pasted and printed out. Now a big proportion of designing, publishing and printing, incorporating magazines, books, poster advertisements, product packaging and other promotional imagery, and a fair amount of television and film production, is the responsibility of people who are familiar with computer technology.

Some media workers have capitalised on new developments by creating their own industry. Interactive multimedia packages which bring a new dimension to global publishing are complemented by another wave of advanced computer programming techniques which enable professionals, such as architects and engineers, to create 3D representations of proposed designs. Now it is possible to walk through a space not yet created. Another part of the computer revolution, the information superhighway, or Internet, is changing the way we access information and communicate with each other. The Internet is used by journalists as a source of newsworthy stories, but it is also beginning to provide a number of employment opportunities in its own right, particularly for those with a specialist knowledge of the subject. Marketing agencies are becoming increasingly interested in what must appear to them to be the new frontier.

Broadcasters have faced some of the greatest challenges to their own status quo recently. The BBC has to justify its existence far more than it ever did in the past. Not content with simply renewing the BBC's licence, the government has demanded a shake-up. Producer choice allows programme makers to buy in facilities from outside, if it is cost-effective to do so, and the BBC must fill 25 per cent of its programming schedule with material

Introduction

bought in from independent companies. The Independent Television (ITV) companies have not escaped the new thinking either. Now that acquisitions and mergers are possible between regional TV companies, single organisations have cut costs, and increased profits and share prices, by laying off staff and amalgamating departments. Radio is also changing and fans of Radio 3 and Radio 4 seem to fight a continuous battle to save the 'integrity' of what they consider to be 'their' station, with competition from the rival commercial station, Classic FM, driving a wedge between traditionalists and popularists.

Not all media jobs are prone to such wild fluctuations, however, and although many of the positions described in this book carry with them a certain amount of stress, not all media jobs are stressful, at least no more so than many other jobs. And while an overview is a useful way to explore the general conditions of the media industry, it is not wholly representative. Most of the jobs described in the following chapters have the same basic components as they always did. Newspaper reporters still report, film directors still direct and so on. So while you may find your industry changes around you, your basic skills, as long as you can adapt them to new situations, will always be needed. This does not mean that there is full employment in the media sector – far from it. There is great competition for places and some sectors, such as the theatre, have a continually shifting workforce which means that unemployment at certain periods is almost inevitable.

For ease of use, this book is separated into broad fields within media. Each chapter explores one part of the media industry, providing job descriptions, employment possibilities, details of desired or necessary qualifications and general information that will assist your search for a career. This book is only intended as a starting point and anyone interested in entering one of the careers mentioned should not regard the text as the be all and end all in careers advice. Instead, the book describes the choices available to you and provides the necessary information with which you can find out more about whatever it is that interests you. The book gives no insight into what it is actually like doing any of the jobs described and for that you should turn to the books in the Kogan Page 'Careers in' series.

At the end of each chapter, there are examples of the courses available, and lists of useful addresses and further reading. All the organisations listed are able to provide you with some careers assistance, be it in the form of a regularly updated, free pamphlet, a magazine which is sold to subscribers, an annual publication or even as a response to a direct letter or telephone call. If you do write to any of these organisations, it is essential to enclose a stamped addressed envelope (SAE).

Job Opportunities

You don't have to move to London to find a job in the media. While it is true that the national newspapers, the BBC, many of the larger publishing houses and the biggest advertising agencies, to name but a few, are based in London, there are hundreds of provincial newspapers, theatres, advertising agencies, printers, independent video companies, graphic designers and so on elsewhere. There is a country-wide network of local radio stations and 15 regional television companies (although some of these have merged into one organisation). EMAP, one of the largest magazine publishers, is based in Peterborough; two excellent British films, *Shallow Grave* and *Trainspotting* came from Scotland not England; one of the most successful small touring theatre companies is based in Hull; Manchester is the home of Coronation Street, Take That and Mark Radcliffe, and the rising star of British performance poetry, Simon Armitage, comes from Huddersfield. You don't even have to be based in or near a city. Freelance writers can work wherever there's a place to put their typewriter or, more likely these days, a plug for their lap-top computer. While Damien Hirst grabs all the headlines for his London exhibitions of fine art, displaying the pickled remains of animals for example, Andy Gallsworthy has gained recognition for his nature-based sculptures, which are made up of leaves, stones, rushes and other natural ingredients set in the place they were found.

Although artists like Damien Hirst inevitably work freelance, it is not necessarily an option open to most of us. Journalism, advertising, arts administration, publishing and printing are all areas which rely on full-time salaried employees. Freelance work is mostly available only to people with years of experience. However, there is almost no salaried work for performers, artists, writers, film and video workers, and in various other specialist occupations.

If you are making the transition from salaried to freelance status, plan the move carefully; build up as wide a range of contacts as you can; assemble a portfolio (or other evidence) of your best work; consider employing an agent and an accountant; find out from your local job centre, or the Benefits Agency, what your rights and obligations are; and take advice on such matters as insurance and pension plans.

As most full-time salaried work is based on short-term contracts which last anything from six months to five years, the difference between freelance work and salaried employment is no longer as great as it once was. Even so, there are pitfalls to avoid. It is very easy to take on too much, or the wrong type of work, because you are afraid to turn down a job and risk losing a potentially useful contact, or because you are worried about not making enough money.

Languages, the Single Market in Europe and Other Overseas Employment

It is not as easy to work overseas, outside the European Union (EU), as it used to be. Residence visas and work permits are required by most countries, and they are only likely to look favourably on people whose skills they need, if there is a shortage of suitably qualified nationals. Short-term overseas employment is common for foreign correspondents, top sports reporters and some performers. Occasionally, designers, illustrators, writers, film-makers and a few other select media workers make a name for themselves in a particular field, find themselves in demand and have to move to another country because the development of their career depends on them being part of a cultural scene. Employees of large multinational companies who work overseas permanently are mainly marketing executives who may be responsible for one enormous area, such as the whole of South East Asia. Some experienced media workers are employed by aid agencies, such as the VSO (Voluntary Service Overseas), ODA (Overseas Development Administration), the UN and others.

Closer to home, many companies will become more involved with Europe as a result of the single market, which will remove all barriers to trade within the EU, and allows the free movement of goods, services, capital and people. It also allows professional qualifications gained in one country to be recognised in another. However, these qualifications may not be enough to clinch a job across the Channel if the candidate does not have the necessary language skills. The basic freedoms of the single market will soon be extended to European countries outside the EU who form part of a wider group of states, known as the European Economic Area. This will allow British nationals to move freely between 28 countries. In all these countries a qualified professional of one member state is recognised as a fully qualified professional in another.

Having said this, British professionals tend to be at a disadvantage unless they have several years' working experience. This is because recent graduates, of whom only 2 per cent start their working lives in Europe, complete degree courses which are much shorter than their European counterparts. For this reason those teaching English in Europe tend to make up most of that 2 per cent. As there is an increasing demand for graduates who can operate at a European level, students should consider taking a course with a European component.

UK ERASMUS (European Community Action Scheme for the Mobility of University Students), now part of the new SOCRATES programme, helps students to study in other EU countries for periods of 3–12 months. Information on job vacancies within the EU is handled by the Overseas Placing Unit in Sheffield, and adverts are placed in most job centres. Anyone considering studying or working abroad should consider contacting the Central Bureau for Educational Visits and Exchanges. They publish a number of useful books and pamphlets and will help you get to grips with new training programmes such as Leonardo da Vinci.

Chapter 1

Broadcasting

Introduction

Anybody can say that they want to work in television or radio; the problem is that there are thousands of people with the same vague 'media' ambitions, many of whom would happily sell their grandparents to secure their first job.

The current jobs climate isn't encouraging. Both the BBC and ITV companies have slimmed down their operations, relying far more heavily on the independent sector to come up with new television ideas and productions. This is largely because they are now legally obliged to commission at least 25 per cent of programming from independent production companies.

Satellite and cable television continue to grow, and in radio there is a batch of new independent sector broadcasters, like Classic FM, Virgin Radio and Atlantic 252. Although all who compete for media jobs are up against stiff opposition, opportunities do still exist – the trick is knowing where to look for them and how to make the most of them when they turn up.

The Employers

The BBC

The BBC is by far the biggest employer, operating two national television channels, five national radio stations, 42 local radio stations, the World Service, the Open University Production Centre and a number of commercial services such as publishing, Worldwide Learning and World TV.

Although most BBC employees are London-based, a quarter of all staff are employed in regional broadcasting, either in Scotland,

Wales and Northern Ireland, or in England in the North, Midlands and East, and South.

As part of an overall efficiency drive, the BBC now only employs a core number of permanent staff, recruiting further numbers on fixed-term contracts, as work demands. Producers have the choice to buy in resources and are no longer obliged to use BBC services if a more cost-effective facility is available elsewhere.

The BBC still offers a number of training programmes in journalism, computing, news, sound, studio management, production and engineering. These schemes are highly regarded and each place has hundreds of applicants. Details from BBC Corporate Recruitment Services.

Ceefax is produced by BBC News and Current Affairs. Again, there are some staff opportunities.

The Independent Television Network (ITV)

Of the 15 regional ITV companies, Carlton, Central, Granada, LWT and Yorkshire broadcast to the most densely populated areas. They provide most of the network's drama and entertainment programming, and production jobs in any of these companies are likely to be highly specialised.

The smallest companies tend to concentrate on regional material and can offer excellent work experience because they are able to give their staff more involvement in a wider range of tasks. Carlton, Meridian and Westcountry are primarily 'publisher broadcasters', which means that they commission independent production companies to make most of their programmes. Legislation changes announced in 1993 allowed, for the first time, two large ITV franchise holders to be owned by the same group or company. This led to a spate of mergers and takeovers and the loss of hundreds of jobs, many ex-employees going on to work for independent production companies.

In September 1996 Granada launched a new initiative for 65 newcomers to television work. The new recruits come from a variety of backgrounds but all have some media experience. They have been recruited to make low-budget but original programming for Granada Sky Broadcasting and none has any previous professional television experience.

Other Television Companies

Channel Four
This channel offers a limited range of jobs because all the programmes it broadcasts are made by independent production companies. However, it does employ managers, engineers, commissioning editors, design and sales staff, continuity announcers, secretaries and computer operators.

The Welsh Fourth Channel (S4C)
S4C schedules 34 hours a week of Welsh language programmes supplied by outside bodies. Of the 100 people it employs, approximately 34 per cent are engineers and 21 per cent work in legal and finance departments. Knowledge of Welsh is essential in areas such as commissioning, presentation, and press and public relations.

Independent Television News (ITN)
ITN provides news programmes to the ITV companies. The company also makes one-off documentaries and broadcasts live 'special event' programmes, such as election night coverage. It employs experienced journalists only.

British Sky Broadcasting (BSkyB)
This recruits staff at all levels, including junior secretarial and administrative posts for school-leavers and technical and production jobs for trained staff. Sky News, Sky Sports, Sky Travel, UK Living, the Discovery Channel, the Family Channel, TLC, the Disney Channel, TCC, the History Channel, Nickelodeon, MTV Europe and VH-1 all produce or commission a proportion of original programming.

Cable TV
Cable TV reaches over 10 million homes but there are still only three main programming companies: United Artists Programming, European Television Networks and BSkyB. Further information about the cable industry is available from the Cable Communications Association.

Working in the Media

Independent Television Production Companies
These companies produce dramas, documentaries, commercials and all the other major TV genres for broadcasting organisations. Many operate with a skeleton crew, buying in labour when it is needed. A few have their own full-time technical and production staff. For information, contact the Producers' Alliance for Cinema and Television (PACT).

Teletext provides text information services for ITV and Channel Four. Based in London it employs roughly 90 full-time staff and some freelance writers.

Independent Radio

There are a number of mainstream national radio stations and a few more which broadcast to a substantial area. Employment is usually for a mixture of full-time staff and freelances. Two of the best known are:

Classic FM
This has a permanent staff of approximately 65, in areas such as programming, sales, finance and marketing, and employs a further 30 freelances on a regular basis. The station offers no sponsorships or work experience and has no training programmes.

Virgin Radio
Virgin Radio employs 55 people, including DJs, producers, accountants and sales and promotional staff. The station's news bulletins are supplied by Reuters.

Independent Local Radio

ILR stations number about 160. (A complete list appears in *Careers in Television and Radio*, published by Kogan Page.) Employment profiles vary from company to company, although every station is staffed by a mix of salaried employees and freelances with full time staff. Each one will have presenters, a programme controller, a head of music, engineers, sales staff and administrative support personnel. Many jobs go to known people so getting contacts will help you obtain work. Training is limited as stations prefer to recruit experienced personnel and give them supplementary, on-the-job training when it is needed.

Broadcasting

Regional ILR Services
These are a relatively new development. Covering larger areas than traditional ILR services they are broadcast in addition to the existing companies in those regions. Five licences have been awarded (for Central Scotland, North East England, North West England, the Severn estuary and the West Midlands) and more are planned. Contact the Association of Independent Radio Companies (AIRC) for details.

Community Radio Stations
These stations are locally owned and not run for commercial profit. The seven fully licensed community-based radio stations are Community Radio Milton Keynes (CRMK), Heartland FM, Radio Maldwyn, Radio Thamesmead (RTM), Townland Radio, Radio Ceredigion and North East Community Radio. Contact the Community Radio Association (CRA) for details.

The Services Sound and Vision Corporation (SSVC)
This is a non-profit-making organisation funded by the Ministry of Defence, which provides the armed forces with a range of entertainment, engineering support and training services. Its broadcasting division comprises SSVC Television and the British Forces Broadcasting Service (BFBS). All SSVC staff (there are 200 employed worldwide) are civilian.

Broadcasting Jobs

Accountants

Accountants are influential players in the broadcasting industry. Financial accountants help to prepare and control company and departmental budgets, provide financial reports and audits, and supervise payments. Programme accountants provide management with information on the state of programme budgets, often working closely with programme directors.

Airtime Sales Staff

These people sell advertising space. Sales co-ordinators negotiate the sale of airtime, take bookings and see that 'slots' are filled; sales executives attract new business; sales research staff carry out and interpret market research; traffic staff monitor the receipt and delivery of advertisements. Trainees are recruited externally and applicants should have good A levels, a degree or equivalent. Advertising agency experience would be beneficial.

Announcers

Announcers provide continuity between programmes. They also project the image of the station. Announcers should have a well-modulated voice, a warm, friendly personality and, for television, an attractive appearance. Announcers write their own scripts, perform occasional interviews, read scripted commentaries, news bulletins and even short advertisements. Most have previous media experience.

Camera Operators

Camera operators are recruited at 18 or over and trained on the job. Applicants should have a good general education, GCSEs in English, maths and preferably a science, and possess some knowledge of optics, film and television photography. They must have normal colour vision and a good eye for picture composition. The work is tiring, the hours often antisocial and much of the work is away from home.

Casting Directors

These directors liaise with agents, visit drama schools and spend time interviewing and auditioning hopefuls. They need a good memory for faces and an instinctive knowledge of who will be right for a certain part. Casting directors are usually experienced professionals.

Continuity Person

Such a person is employed to ensure that every detail of dress, the set and the story remains consistent from scene to scene so the programme looks as though it was filmed in one go. Often this job goes to production assistants with an eye for detail and a regard for accuracy.

Broadcasting

Costume Design Assistants

These people arrange fittings, research designs and shop for fabrics. Applicants normally hold a degree or equivalent qualification in theatrical or fashion design and have had professional experience.

Costume Designers

Costume designers working in entertainment and drama read the script, liaise with the other production staff and work out the costume budget. Costume designers should have a good grounding in the history of costume, be creative and innovative and possess administrative and supervisory skills.

DJs

These jobs are sought after, and radio stations receive hundreds of unsolicited applications and demo tapes every year. Presenters need to possess an easy microphone manner, a grasp of current affairs, a pleasant voice and the ability to think quickly and to ad lib when necessary. On local radio stations they will also need good technical skills. Generally speaking, presenters will start off in university, hospital or community radio, move on to local radio and, if they are like Chris Evans, find their way to national fame and fortune.

Dressers

Dressers maintain costumes and carry out minor alterations, so they must be able to sew quickly and neatly. They also need tact, maturity and sensitivity as they help artists on and off with their costumes. People under the age of 20 are rarely recruited for this work.

Dressmakers

Dressmakers work on any kind of costume, making their own patterns from the designer's working drawings. With basic training in pattern-making, cutting and dressmaking to BTEC HND level, a dressmaker will start out by getting work experience with a fashion house or theatrical costumier.

Editors

Editors work closely with the producer and director as they prepare the final version of the programme. The editor is responsible for cutting together images so the programme makes logical sense and fulfils design criteria such as 'eye-catching', 'dramatic', and so on. The work demands great attention to detail, precision and creativity and these skills take a long time to accumulate. Ironically, the better the editor, the less conscious the viewer will be of his or her work.

Electronic News Gathering (ENG) Editors

These editors have to meet deadlines for news bulletins and are usually working under great pressure. They maintain and repair their own equipment and mainly work away from the studio.

Film and Videotape Librarians

These people need a knowledge of production, storage and handling techniques and can be asked to do simple editing jobs. There are a number of posts for graduate chartered librarians, assistant librarians and clerical library assistants.

Floor Managers

Floor managers are responsible for everything that happens on the studio floor: they check that props are in place, make sure performers know where to stand and what to do, give prompts and look after the studio audience, if there is one. They are constantly in touch with the programme director, who watches the proceedings from a production gallery. Floor managers must be organised, calm and tactful. Trainees should have had a good general education to at least GCSE (grade C) or equivalent standard, and experience of working in the theatre.

Graphic Designers

Graphic designers are responsible for designing and supervising the execution of all graphic programme material, including credits, charts, graphs, logos and even some props, such as documents used in drama. Working in close consultation with the other members of the production staff the graphic designer must be capable of turning concepts into design realities.

Journalists and Other Newsroom Staff

These people work under intense pressure to meet strict deadlines. In broadcasting, journalists can become news editors, news readers or special correspondents. Fierce competition makes a degree an almost inevitable requirement and although it is possible to learn some of the skills needed for broadcast journalism, some people will have an obvious talent for writing and presentation. For more details, see Chapter 7.

All journalists receive some legal training but legal expertise is also required in the contracts department and in fields such as libel law and court reporting.

Lighting Directors

Lighting directors create atmosphere. In a chat show this would be comparatively straightforward and in a drama quite complex. They liaise with the rest of the production team and prepare plans for, and supervise the work of, the lighting electricians and lighting console operators.

Lighting or Production Electricians

These electricians work according to the specifications of the lighting director, arranging studio lamps on the lighting grid in the studio roof. They also repair and maintain the apparatus they use, so a good head for heights is essential.

Location Managers

Location managers are most commonly found working in drama productions where they find suitable sites for filming and arrange practical matters regarding a shoot in the particular location they have chosen. This would include getting permission for filming, sorting out a contract with the land or property owner and making sure the site is as it was when the film crew moved in.

Make-up Artists

Make-up artists spend most of their time doing corrective work like powdering noses or taking the shine off bald patches so they probably yearn for more creative tasks. Producing a Freddie Kruger or an Edward Scissorhands is an art which takes great patience. As they work with many different sorts of people, a calm, tactful personality helps. Make-up artists start as trainees and general requirements include normal colour vision, a good general education (A levels in English, art and history are particularly desirable) and recognised qualifications in make-up and/or hairdressing, and/or beauty culture.

Operational Engineers

Operational engineers are responsible for the technical facilities needed for the production and transmission of programmes and may be involved in studio work and outside broadcasts as well as the operation and maintenance of the networks, and transmission systems.

Performers

Performers rarely find permanent full-time employment and only 25 per cent of Equity's 30,000 members are working at any one time. If you feel dedicated, read Chapter 3.

Presenters

Presenters' jobs are rarely advertised. This is because most presenters are approached and offered a contract; many are well known in another field already and others come from a local radio background.

Producers

Producers turn their own ideas into programmes. They head the production team and are responsible for managing the programme budget and the scheduling of rehearsal and recording time. Radio producers often record material as well, although these duties may be shared with a researcher and production assistant. Producers must understand the requirements of the network or region in which they are working. Generally speaking, they specialise in one subject.

Production Assistants (PAs)

PAs work on a particular programme from start to finish, providing support for the producer and director. They attend all the programme planning meetings and carry out any duties which they are assigned. In the final run-through of a television production the PA

Broadcasting

sits with the director in the control room and instructs the camera operators. The job requires excellent organisational skills, attention to detail, calm, initiative and the ability to manage and get on with all types of people. Most PAs are recruited as trainees and many traineeships are filled by people already in broadcasting.

Programme Assistants

Programme assistants are responsible for the technical and artistic presentation of programmes. They need to be able to operate the equipment and to be good at dealing with other people in the team and with the people who are interviewed. This job is often seen as a first step for people wanting to get into radio production work. A PA on a local radio station will provide the presenter with full production support, before and throughout the programme. Many people become PAs after spending time as a volunteer, or contributing to programming in some other way.

Programme Directors

Programme directors place the actors and discuss their interpretation of the roles and, after consultation with the technical experts, decide on lighting effects, camera angles and so on. When shooting has been completed, the director supervises post-production work, such as editing and sound dubbing. In radio drama, the director rehearses the actors, selects sound effects and, again, supervises post-production. Becoming a director is not easy as most vacancies are filled by internal applicants with substantial production experience.

Property Staff

Property staff work with props. A buyer will make sure a TV production gets the props it needs and once on set the property staff will work with the stage hands to ensure property is well maintained. Theatrical experience is an advantage, but vacancies are rare.

Researchers

Researchers provide the necessary depth to programmes and successful ones will have a hard-working, competent employee

Working in the Media

lining up and interviewing contacts, conducting vox pops, finding locations, digging through statistical information, checking through archives and scriptwriting. There is stiff competition for jobs and successful applicants are usually in their twenties, hold a good degree and have some kind of media-related experience.

Script Editors

Script editors commission writers, find new writing talent, conduct research and rewrite material. In a long-running series, the script editor ensures that each episode is written in a uniform style. The script editor may also develop storylines. Essential qualities for the job are tact, patience, an excellent memory and a genuine love of reading and drama. Script editors generally have a literary background and have worked in the theatre.

Secretarial

Secretarial positions are often viewed as a way into the media and attract a high proportion of graduate applicants, hoping to find their way to production posts. However, competition for production posts is extremely tough and secretarial experience is not often good enough. In addition, all staff are expected to remain in their first post for a reasonable length of time before applying for a transfer.

Set Designers

Set designers working for TV, unlike their theatrical counterparts, have to consider cameras, cables and microphone booms in their designs. Apart from that, the jobs are quite similar.

Sound Mixers

Sound mixers monitor and balance the sound signals from a control room, feeding in sound effects and music when appropriate.

Sound Operators

Sound operators balance, mix and record sound if they work in a radio studio. In television, they ensure that the studio equipment is working and that the microphone boom arms are effectively positioned. They also edit taped speech and music and select sound effects. On outside broadcasts they will be responsible for rigging up and dismantling equipment. Applicants should be aged 18 or over, have normal hearing and colour vision and have had a good general education.

Specialist Engineers

These engineers work in research and design, developing new techniques and improving existing equipment.

Stagehands

Also known as 'setting assistants', stagehands usually come from a craft background and have theatrical training. No special educational qualifications are needed but shifting scenery often takes precision timing and a lot of common sense. A clean driving licence is also useful.

Stage Managers

Stage managers organise rehearsals, ensuring they run as smoothly as possible. All stage managers have had previous experience of theatre or television.

Trainee Engineers

Trainee engineers act as a support force for qualified engineers, setting up, aligning and maintaining equipment while they train to become engineers themselves. Applicants for traineeships should be aged between 18 and 26, have normal hearing and colour vision and hold (as minimum qualifications) GCSEs at grades A, B or C or equivalent in English, maths and physics, a BTEC National Certificate or Diploma in electrical engineering, or have studied maths and physics to A level.

Transmission Controllers

Transmission controllers work from a mixer console connected to a bank of television screens, making sure the right programme is 'sent out' at the right time. The work involves a great deal of planning and combines periods of intense activity with periods during which nothing happens. Transmisssion controllers need to be able to think and act quickly if there is a technical failure as they must not leave viewers with a blank screen. Most vacancies are filled internally and trainees are usually aged between

18 and 21. Applicants need normal colour vision, good hearing and a good general education (most hold A levels or a degree).

Vision Mixers

Vision mixers work on the instructions of the director. The console where the mixer works can produce special effects to make the transition from one scene to another more interesting or unobtrusive and, because the mixer is working with a number of different images, quick reactions and excellent timing are required.

Visual Effects Designers

These designers need a good working knowledge of sculpture, model making, painting, optics and pyrotechnics, together with an understanding of the principles of physics, chemistry and electricity. There are few permanent posts in television companies and most work freelance, or for facility houses which provide services for other film and television companies. Art college experience or an electronics qualification and, ideally, experience in films or the theatre will make life easier if you are trying to enter this specialised field.

Wardrobe

These jobs are covered in Chapter 3, page 40.

Weather Forecasts

These are generally prepared and presented by qualified meteorologists, who see radio and television work as only a small part of their job. International Weather Productions and the Weather Department produce weather bulletins for ITV but neither employ many staff and both rely on highly trained and experienced people.

Writing

Writing for broadcast is specialised work, so it is a good idea to learn the techniques. Most TV writers will have read books on the subject or taken a course which sets out the ground rules. Work is seldom full time and writers usually have other work they can rely on to cover the lean months. Chapter 6 contains useful information for all freelance writers.

Getting Started

Competition for media jobs is intense. Many people are so eager to start work they apply for posts that they would not consider accepting in any other sector, just to get in. There are undoubted advantages to this approach. Simply by turning up on time and doing your job you are showing yourself to be dependable and enthusiastic. At the same time you learn how other jobs are done and get to know the names of the key people within the company.

Even getting to this early stage you will probably have to demonstrate a commitment to media work by having a curriculum vitae that contains details of prior experience with a voluntary organisation such as community, campus or hospital radio, or paid work experience with a related media organisation. Good academic qualifications can give you the edge but they are no guarantee of job success. All applicants must be able to work as part of a team, keep a cool head under pressure and communicate well.

Sometimes advertisements for media jobs should carry a government health warning. The competitive atmosphere of a broadcasting company can be emotionally and physically taxing. Lifestyles are generally disruptive to family life and prolonged periods of early rises or late finishes can be very tiring, especially if you are just starting out and are not yet seeing the creative and financial rewards associated with the industry.

If you are undaunted by the health warning, you'll still want to know how to get your first job. The truth is, there are no hard and fast rules on how to 'make it'. Only the most able, creative and enthusiastic are likely to succeed so you must always be realistic about your own abilities.

Think carefully about what you want to do and focus on that goal. If you can't get work experience in radio, you can develop skills in related areas by writing for a local newspaper or school magazine. Critically analyse a wide range of television and radio output and ask yourself why a programme works or why it doesn't, and what you would do to improve it. Go to the library and order some of the books listed in the recommended reading section on page 37 of this book.

If you really want to know how the media works, you need to get proper work experience. Channel Four doesn't offer any and the BBC's policy varies from region to region. Most ITV companies do offer work experience, although they usually insist that applicants are students following a recognised course of study at a college or university. Some independent production companies will also offer work experience placements. The Yellow Pages contains lists of local production companies under the sections TV, Film and Video Production Services and Broadcasting Services.

You will get a good head start if you join a hospital, campus or community radio station. All three provide valuable and prolonged work experience. Many people get their first job by doing voluntary, temporary or part-time work for a local radio station, just by being in the right place at the right time. Even if you don't get paid work, being able to experience such a wide range of programming styles is a great help for future job applications.

Local radio stations are always on the look out for new talent but if you are thinking of sending a demo tape, you should keep it short. An all-rounder's tape could include a news reading, a well-structured interview and a sample of how you introduce music.

Courses and Training Schemes

There are literally hundreds of media-related courses and the essential guide to the subject is *Media Courses UK*, published annually by the British Film Institute. They also publish the *BFI Film and Television Handbook* which contains listings of colleges, workshops, organisations, hire facilities and production companies.

Skillset (the industry training organisation) is developing a course database which they hope to make available via access points around the country. Until then, contact Skillset directly if you want to make a specific inquiry about a course or would like a copy of their careers booklet. The Association of Independent Radio Companies (AIRC) also maintains an extensive database of current training.

It is essential that you take the time to choose the course best suited to you and your interests. Generally speaking, it is best to opt for a course that will give you a solid grounding in practical skills. Industry training is currently being reviewed so that National Vocational Qualifications become the norm. This will standardise on-the-job training, hopefully encouraging employers to offer more training programmes. At the moment, CSV Media, Film and Television Freelance Training (FT2), Scottish Broadcast and Film Training Ltd, Gaelic Television Training Trust and Cyfle (for Welsh speakers) all offer specialised, on-the-job training with a college component.

Courses, Useful Addresses and Further Reading

See pages 31–7 in Chapter 2.

Chapter 2
Film and Video

Introduction

Your first job in the film industry may be the hardest to find. Vacancies for beginners, even those with a film studies degree, are never very numerous. And, depending on the production and economic state of the industry, vacancies may at times be almost non-existent. This is the reality that anyone entering the film and video industry must face. Starting off at the bottom is generally speaking the only way to get to the top. 'Get in any way you can,' advises Mark Samuelson of the Producers' Alliance for Cinema and Television (PACT), 'get any job you can'.

Once in, it's easier to find more work, but quite often periods of intense activity, hard work and stress will be followed by frustrating unemployment, when nothing seems to happen. Few people have regular employment.

Most film and video companies operate with a skeleton staff, employing people when it is necessary. The only permanent staff may be the executive producer and a secretary. The same goes for film studios. For example, Pinewood studios, which produced *Mission Impossible* and *Aliens*, not to mention most of the James Bond films, employs only 140 people, but during a typical day's filming provides work for 2,500.

As most of the activity is based in London there is an obvious advantage to living in the South. Having said this, all regions have their own independent video production companies and a quick glance in the Yellow Pages will indicate the range of services available outside London. Some video companies offer specialist packages to fulfil educational, business and training requirements and it is important to say that not all video and film making is drama or documentary based. Some companies will produce

Film and Video

corporate videos and adverts to promote a particular organisation or product.

Often professionals are hired regularly by a particular director or producer and are able to build up a relationship with other crew members. As employment is only guaranteed while your services are needed, a secondary occupation, which you can fall back on if you have no other work, is useful. Even better, ensure you are highly regarded and much in demand.

The Broadcasting Entertainment Cinematograph and Theatre Union (BECTU) represents the interests of people employed in the industry. Although it is no longer necessary to be a member to get a job, BECTU still offers a number of very good services and sets pay standards across the country. Students can join for £10 a year, a deal which allows access to useful industry information and BECTU's monthly periodical, *Stage, Screen and Radio*.

British films are making something of a comeback at the moment and a number of overseas ventures are producing films on British soil, which are often about British culture or history. The British Film Institute (BFI), the BBC, Channel Four and a number of small independent film producers have created a string of British hits. This, when seen alongside the expanding video and interactive computer market, makes sure the moving image industry in Britain is more positive than it has been for some time. This is reflected by an ever-increasing number of technical and theoretical courses associated with the moving image (see pages 31–4).

The Stages of Film-making

Only a few people work on every stage of the film-making process:

- *Pre-production*. The producer finds funding for the film or video, hires a director, cast and crew. Locations and equipment are arranged; a budget and shooting schedule is prepared.
- *Production*. The film is 'shot', either on location or in the studio.
- *Post-production*. The film is processed, edited and completed with a soundtrack, opticals, titles and special effects. Sometimes this can take longer than the actual filming.

The Producer

The producer is the final authority on all practical matters, including the budget. Quite often the film idea comes from the producer, who sets about obtaining the rights to the property if it is a book or script, or oversees the writing of an original screenplay. The producer then puts the whole package together and monitors the day-to-day progress of the film. The producer must be determined, unwilling to take no for an answer, well organised and shrewd.

The Director

The director decides how best to use the technical and artistic resources available. He or she guides the actors on their interpretation of the part and tells the camera operators what kind of image to shoot. The director must be able to conceptualise a script and visualise it, using certain images, effects and sounds. Although the director is in complete control of the filming, and determines the film's artistic content, he or she does not always have the final say on all creative matters. If a producer is not happy with the final cut, changes may have to be made by the director.

Continuity Personnel

Continuity personnel make certain that everything, from position of props and clothing to gestures and voice inflections, matches from one shot to the next. Working closely with the director, continuity personnel make sure that the film looks as if it was shot all at once. This is a job for someone with a highly developed sense of observation.

The Production Manager

The production manager has overall responsibility for the organisation of the picture and is the producer's deputy, preparing a detailed budget and schedule for shooting, supervising the smooth running of the shoot, sorting out contracts, hiring equipment, and obtaining permission for location shoots.

The Assistant Director

He or she ensures that the director's instructions are carried out correctly, particularly important when the film costs £40 million.

Film and Video

There are usually three assistants. The first assistant anticipates and carries out the director's practical requirements, generally organising the daily shooting schedule, liaising with the production manager and providing an important link between the production department and the director. The first assistant also hires the second and third assistants, usually people who are known to be good at their job. The second assistant works with the production office and the third assistant works on the set. Both act as the legs of the first assistant. The assistant directors are often a barometer of the crew's feelings, letting the director know when the crew is tired or dissatisfied. They are there to maximise the efficiency of the film unit, making sure that no time is wasted.

The Cinematographer *or* Director of Photography

This person is, after the director, the most creative member of the team. Responsible for lighting each shot, choosing camera angles, lenses and filters, the cinematographer decides how each shot should look and how best to interpret the director's intentions.

The Camera Operator

The Camera Operator and the cinematographer often work as a team, going from one production to the next. The operator handles the camera and is responsible for a smooth and efficient camera movement. The camera operator will work with a focus puller, who controls the focus of the camera, and the clapper/loader, who loads the film into the camera, operates the clapper board before each shot and keeps a record of all filming.

The Sound Department

This department will have a sound mixer and sound recordist, both of whom work on location, a boom handler to control the microphones and a dubbing mixer who supervises the recording of additional sound, including music and sound effects. The dubbing mixer must also match the image on screen to the sound recording, a highly technical and creative job which takes years of practice.

Working in the Media

The Editor

The editor determines the narrative structure of the film by cutting, editing and assembling the picture. Most of the work is done in post-production and the editor's skill can make or break a picture. The editor usually has two assistants who collect the rushes, put location sound to picture for viewing and join the cuts together under the supervision of the editor.

The Studio Floor Manager

The studio floor manager acts as a link between the floor and the director, to organise the sequences of the shoot. He or she needs to be tactful, assertive, calm and confident (see also Chapter 1, p.14).

There is also a wide range of related occupations that make films happen, including carpenters, metal workers, electricians and engineers. The work is always occasional but well paid, and it can involve interesting locations and unusual challenges. For example, the producers of *First Knight*, which was filmed in Wales, hired a small army of carpenters to create a plywood Camelot, the image of which was later enhanced in post-production with the aid of computer graphics.

Getting Started

Only a few positions are advertised in magazines or newspapers. Most people find out about jobs through word of mouth. The more people you know, the better your chances of employment – so a lot of it comes down to making your own luck.

Film course students will probably meet up with potential employers during the course of their studies and it may be a good idea to join one of the film organisations to go to lectures and seminars. When you meet someone working in film always take their name and ask if it would be convenient to call.

The companies involved in the film industry change from year to year and those publications which provide relatively up-to-date information about the various production and post-production companies are *The Broadcast Production Guide*, *Kemp's International Film and Television Yearbook* and *The Knowledge*, or *PACT Members' Directory*. All should be available from most public libraries.

Film and Video

Becoming a runner or messenger, the traditional way to start off in the film industry, is still a popular choice among new entrants because of the experience and contacts it provides. Production and post-production companies usually have one or two runners on their staff. They also often hire runners during the actual production. Most companies prefer someone young, about 16 or 17. They do not pay very well and it is hard work. As the openings are rarely advertised, you have to write to or telephone the various companies, or appear in person, asking about jobs.

From a messenger, you can usually become an assistant or a trainee but as the messenger period is intended as an apprenticeship for you to learn more about the industry and the company you work for, do not expect to be moved up within a few months. You may also find work as a secretary or receptionist with a production company, which could lead to the possibility of moving into production work. Most companies prefer someone aged 18 or older with good typing and shorthand skills. These jobs are advertised through local papers, The *Guardian*, various media publications and also through special agencies.

If you have completed a film or television course, your chances of getting a trainee position are much improved. Some film schools produce work for broadcast or viewing. These screenings often lead to more work. One video film-maker in Nottingham made his first film 'short' by himself, playing all the parts, producing and directing, all with a hand-held camcorder borrowed from a local arts organisation. By the time he wanted to make his second film, he had recruited a number of friends to help him out. Using this film, he managed to get funding for a third film, which won an award, and brought him to the attention of Stephen Frear. With the assistance of this established director he is producing his first full-length film, taking some of his own production crew with him.

The maker of *Hear My Song* directed his first film, a short called *Treacle*, with the assistance of the BBC, who funded the project as part of a competition for new directors called 10 x 10. The BBC offered a £50,000 budget and insisted that the film was no more than 10 minutes long. His second film was the British-made movie *Hear My Song* and his third film (*Funny Bones*), backed by Hollywood, starred Jerry Lewis as an ageing American comedian re-evaluating his past in Blackpool. Making a short film is a good way of exploring your own talents and capabilities before moving on to bigger films. There are a number of awards and competitions for shorts and those interested in finding out about them should contact the BFI, Channel 4 and the BBC.

Regional arts organisations are often prepared to sponsor talented film-makers, if it will assist their career aims. Funding is usually quite small but enough to allow you to make a very low-budget film or video. Getting material together is very important and learning to use available resources wisely and efficiently is an important skill to learn. A short, with a good story and interesting camera work, can make up for a lack of money. There may also be a local arts organisation which can provide you with technical assistance and equipment. You may find other people there who want to make films. Similarly, a conference or weekend course can often be advantageous. Useful contacts are made at these events, which are often listed in the industry magazines.

Education and Training

Training for film work is slowly changing. Traditionally, training was acquired on the job, in a haphazard and fragmented way: you started by making the tea and worked your way up. Now it is possible to get formal training from an art college or university. Alternatively, you can study for an NVQ qualification while working.

Skillset is the industry training organisation for broadcast, film and video. It publishes a careers pack containing details of training opportunities which is available by sending an A4 SAE. Film and Television Freelance Training (FT2) trains technicians for the freelance film and television industry. Known as New Entrant Training, the programme is an apprenticeship scheme, with trainees attached to various productions over a two-year training period. This is supported by specially commissioned courses at colleges and training centres. They do not train directors, producers or scriptwriters.

Film School

There are a number of reasons for continuing your studies at film school. Because competition for jobs is fierce, the more know-

Film and Video

ledgeable and experienced you are the better. Film studies will give you practical experience in production and familiarise you with new technology and equipment. Most importantly, you are likely to meet other members of the film industry. However, it cannot be stressed enough that no school can guarantee employment. BECTU recognises that the education and training received at specific schools is equal to an apprenticeship as a messenger or runner. They feel that completion of a three-year, full-time course is equal to intensive practical training. The National Film and Television School at Beaconsfield in Buckinghamshire is undoubtedly the best film school in Britain.

There is no official accreditation scheme for film schools any more so it isn't easy to pick out the right one. Some of the more established schools will carry recommendations from those in the industry but the number of new courses springing up each year makes this choice less straightforward.

Visit the educational establishment you are considering and talk to the students already there. Ask the course administrator what has happened to previous students since they left the course. Look over the equipment and find out how much time you will spend using it, and whether they will train you to operate all the equipment you see. Find out what industry experience course tutors have and whether work placements will be a part of the course.

The competition for places is tough and you should apply early. You will need a sample of previous work, such as a short film or a script. Applicants must be at least 18 years old and possess five GCSE passes, two of which should be at A level.

Courses

As many of the technical and creative courses are appropriate for both the broadcasting and film and video sectors, they are listed here together. For more details, order a copy of *Media Courses UK* from the British Film Institute. Other useful contacts are Skillset, BECTU, Scottish Broadcast and Film Training, the Gaelic Television Training Trust, Cyfle (for Welsh speakers) and the Association of Independent Radio Companies (AIRC).

A number of media studies courses have sprung up in recent years. Although they may offer useful formative training for careers in the media, they are not specifically vocational and few are officially recognised for accreditation by the professional organisations or unions. Although employers will see media studies as a useful grounding, they will not recognise the courses as offering the specific, in-depth technical training which other courses can offer.

There are over 100 colleges offering BTEC/SCOTVEC, HND/C, GNVQ Advanced or City & Guilds courses related to the teaching of production techniques, including sound, lighting, electronics and engineering. A complete list can be found in *Media Courses UK*.

Degree Level Qualifications

Video Production, the American College in London
Media Production, Bournemouth University, Farnborough College of Technology, University of Humberside, University of Luton, University of Northumbria, South East Essex College of Arts and Technology,
Costume for the Screen and Stage, Bournemouth University
Scriptwriting for Film and Television, Bournemouth University
Visual Communication, Brunel University, University of Central England in Birmingham, Coventry University, Edinburgh College of Art, Goldsmiths College, Kent Institute of Art and Design, Maidstone College, University of Ulster
Combined Studies, Canterbury Christ Church College of Higher Education
Photography, Film and Television, University of Central London, Napier University
Fine Art (also relevant for designers), Central Saint Martin's College of Art and Design, University of East London, Nottingham Trent University, Sheffield Hallam University
Media Studies, De Montfort University, Sheffield Hallam, University of Stirling, University of Sunderland, University of Sussex, Wirral Metropolitan College
Photographic Studies, University of Derby (includes film and video)
Theatre and Media Drama, University of Glamorgan, King Alfred's College of Higher Education
Graphic Design, (also relevant for designers), Glasgow School of Art, University of Humberside, Kingston University, Norwich School of Art and Design, University of Portsmouth
Broadcasting, University of Leeds

Film and Video

Media Technology, Leeds Metropolitan University
Film and Video, London College of Printing and Distributive Trades, Surrey Institute of Art and Design
Documentary Production, University of Humberside
European Audio-Visual Production, University of Humberside
Screen Studies, Liverpool John Moores University
Interactive and Broadcast Media, Manchester Metropolitan University
MediaLab Arts, University of Plymouth
Film and Television Production, Salisbury College
Television and Radio, University College Salford
Film, Television, Literature and Theatre Studies, University College of Ripon and York St John
Time-based Media, University of the West of England
Contemporary Media Practice, University of Westminster

Some of the academic institutions listed above offer postgraduate courses but there are a few not mentioned which also, or only, offer postgraduate courses. These are: London International Film School, National Film and Television School, Northern Media School, Northern School of Film and Television, Royal College of Art, Scottish Film School, University of Wales.

Other Training Schemes

CSV Media works in partnership with over 100 local TV and radio stations to provide nationally validated training programmes in a range of media skills for unemployed young people and adults.

European Media School provides training in many aspects of media production and management. Students are chosen competitively on the basis of talent, enthusiasm and commitment.

Scottish Broadcast and Film Training Ltd is an employer-led partnership operating in Scotland. It runs a New Entrants Scheme which provides eight, 18-month training places across production, craft and creative areas for young people over the age of 18.

Gaelic Television Training Trust offers a two-year programme of college and industry-based training to Gaelic speakers. Based on the Isle of Skye.

Cyfle provides training for Welsh speakers in the film and television industry. It is a two-year, full-time course involving placements with independent production companies in Wales as well as formal training sessions and seminars.

There are a number of organisations offering specific **training for women** through short courses. They are: Cambridge Women's Resource Centre, 01223 321148; Leeds Animation Workshop, 0113 248 4997; Second Sight, 0121 622 4223; WHEEL (Women's Health, Education and Leisure), 0171 831 6946; WITCH (Women's Independent Cinema House), 0151 707 0539; Women in Film and Television, 0171 379 0344; Women's Media Resource Project, 0171 253 6536.

For hairdressing and make-up, the Retford International College has two courses: Film and Television Make-Up, Hair Design, Wigmaking and Special Effects Course and Make-Up and Hairdressing – Total Look Fashion. Its address is 25–27 Bridgegate, Retford, Nottinghamshire, DN22 7UX; 01777 707371.

Short courses in film and video production techniques are available all over the country and many are listed in *Media Courses UK* (BFI) and *Careers in Film and Video* (Kogan Page).

Useful Addresses

BBC

BBC Corporate Recruitment Services, White City, Wood Lane, London W12 7TS; 0181 752 5252

BBC Radios 1, 2, 3, 4 and 5 Live, Broadcasting House, Portland Place, London W1A 1AA; 0171 580 4468

BBC Television Centre, Wood Lane, London W12 7RJ; 0181 743 8000

BBC World Service, Bush House, Strand, London WC2B 4PH; 0171 240 3456

ITV

Carlton/Central, The Television House, Lenton Lane, Nottingham NG7 2NA; 0115 986 3322

Granada Television Ltd, Quay Street, Manchester M60 9EA; 0161 832 7211

Independent Television News, 200 Gray's Inn Road, London WC1X 8FH; 0171 833 3000

Film and Video

ITV Network Centre, 200 Gray's Inn Road, London WC1X 8FH; 0171 843 8000

London News Network (LNN), The London Television Centre, Upper Ground, London SE1 9LT; 0171 827 7700

London Weekend Television (LWT), The London Television Centre, Upper Ground, London SE1 9LT; 0171 620 1620

Meridian Broadcasting Ltd, Television Centre, Southampton SO14 0PZ; 01703 222555

Scottish Television plc, Cowcaddens, Glasgow G2 3PR; 0141 300 3000

Teletext Ltd, 101 Farm Lane, London SW6 1QJ; 0171 386 5000

Westcountry Television Ltd, Western Wood Way, Language Science Park, Plymouth PL7 5BG; 01752 333333

Yorkshire Television Ltd, The Television Centre, Leeds LS3 1JS; 0113 243 8283

Channel Four and S4C

Channel Four Television, 124 Horseferry Road, London SW1P 2TX; 0171 396 4444

S4C, Parc Ty Glas, Cardiff CF4 5DU; 01222 747444

Independent National Radio

Association of Independent Radio Companies (AIRC), 46 Westbourne Grove, London W2 5SH; 0171 727 2646

Atlantic 252, 74 Newman Street, London W1P 3LA; 0171 436 4012

Classic FM, PO Box 3434, London NW1 7DQ; 0171 284 3000

Talk Radio UK, 76 Oxford Street, London W1N 0TR; 0171 636 1089

Virgin Radio, 1 Golden Square, London W1R 4DJ; 0171 434 1215

British Film Institute (BFI), 21 Stephen Street, London W1P 2LN; 0171 255 1444

British Sky Broadcasting, 6 Centaurs Business Park, Grant Way, Isleworth, Middlesex TW7 5QD; 0171 705 3000

Broadcasting Entertainment Cinematograph and Theatre Union (BECTU), 111 Wardour Street, London W1P 4AY; 0171 437 8506

Cable Communications Association, Fifth Floor, Artillery House, Artillery Row, London SW1P 1RT; 0171 222 2900

Community Radio Association, The Work Station, 15 Paternoster Row, Sheffield S1 2BX; 0114 279 5219
CSV Media, 237 Pentonville Road, London N1 9NJ; 0171 278 6601
Cyfle, Llawr Uchaf, Gronant, Penrallt Isaf, Caernarfon, Gwynnedd LL55 1NW; 01286 671 000
European Media School, Stonehills, Shields Road, Gateshead, Tyne and Wear NE10 0HW; 0191 495 2727
Film and Television Freelance Training (FT2), Fourth Floor, 5 Dean Street, London W1V 5RN; 0171 734 5141
First Film Foundation, 222 Kensal Road, London W10 5BN; 0181 969 5195
Gaelic Television Training Trust, Sabhal Mor Ostaig, Sleat, Isle of Skye IV44 8RQ; 01471 844373
Hospital Broadcasting Association, Staithe House, Russel Street, Falkirk FK2 7HP; 01324 611996
London International Film School, 24 Shelton Street, Covent Garden, London WC2H 9HP; 0171 836 9642
National Council for the Training of Broadcast Journalists, The Secretary, 188 Lichfield Court, Sheen Road, Richmond, Surrey TW9 1BB; 0181 940 0694
National Film and Television School, Beaconsfield Studios, Station Road, Beaconsfield, Buckinghamshire HP9 1LG; 01494 671234
Producers' Alliance for Cinema and Television (PACT), Gordon House, Greencoat Place, London SW1P 1PH; 0171 233 6000
Scottish Broadcast and Film Training Ltd, 4 Park Gardens, Glasgow G3 7YE; 0141 332 2201
The Services Sound and Vision Corporation (SSVC), PO Box 1234, London W2 1XN; 0171 724 1234
Skillset, 124 Horseferry Road, London SW1P 2TX; 0171 306 8585/8547

Further Reading

BFI British Film and TV Handbook, British Film Institute
The Broadcast Production Guide, International Thomson
Careers in Film and Video, Ricki Ostrov and Howard Hall, Kogan Page, 1996
Careers in Television and Radio, Michael Selby, Kogan Page, 1996

Film and Video

Kemp's International Film and Television Yearbook, Reed Information Services
The Knowledge, Miller Freeman Information Services
Lights, Camera Action! Careers in Film, Television and Video, Josephine Langham, British Film Institute, 1993
Media Courses UK 1996, edited by Lavinia Orton, British Film Institute, 1995
Pact Magazine, PACT
PACT Members' Directory, PACT
Screen Digest, 37 Gower Street, London WC1E 6HH; 0171 580 2842
Sight and Sound, British Film Institute,
Stage, Screen and Radio, BECTU
Television, Royal Television Society

Chapter 3
The Theatre and Performance Arts

Backstage

'The world is a stage, the stage is a world of entertainment', or so the song goes. Behind the stage, producers, directors, electricians, designers, all highly skilled individuals, work flat out to ensure the curtain rises when the audience settles and the lights dim. Although it's true that theatre work is not quite like any other job, it isn't always as magical as the cinema might suggest; ask anybody who removes stage sets for a living.

Theatre programmes usually include a list of staff members so it's fairly easy to see who gets employed to do what. Sometimes the lists include departments for voice, casting, scenery, education, wigs and make-up, props, music, construction and so on, but more often than not the numbers who work in any one theatre are actually quite small. Often, several jobs will be done by one person.

The Producer

The producer shoulders the economic and managerial responsibilities of a production, from choosing the play, director and cast, to renting the theatre. The producer has to raise the money (from grants, ticket sales and backers) and balance the budget. There's no specific training but useful qualifications include tact, persuasiveness, a sound business sense, a flair for organisation and an instinct for what it is the public wants.

The Theatre and Performance Arts

The Director

The director masterminds the interpretative approach of the production and has overall responsibility for artistic presentation. Sometimes working with the author, the director will choose cast members and designers, and go on to create a production from nothing. There aren't many training opportunities in professional theatre, but it may be possible to work as an assistant director, helping at rehearsals, doing the director's chores and rehearsing the understudies. Most directors learn by going to drama school, or by taking a drama degree, getting work experience with a theatre company and doing what they can to find their first job.

The Casting Director

He or she works with the producer and director, acting as their talent scout. This means going regularly to drama school productions, interviewing and auditioning hopefuls, and liaising with the agents of more established actors. They must have an excellent memory for faces and an instinctive knowledge of who will be right for a certain part.

The Designer

The designer creates the image for the sets and costumes, either on paper or in the form of a model. A stage designer needs a thorough knowledge of period settings and costumes and must be able to create a stylish and exciting stage set without going over budget. Designers have a college-based education. Entrance requirements range from a portfolio of work and relevant experience to four GCSEs (Grade C or above) for National Diploma courses, plus one A level for Higher National Diploma courses, and five GCSEs and a couple of A levels for degree courses. See also Chapter 9.

The Stage Manager

This job involves organising rehearsals and making sure the performances run smoothly. A stage manager usually has several assistants, known as ASMs (assistant stage managers), as well as (in a large company) a deputy. The team must know the technical cues for scene changes, sound effects, lighting and so on and must be aware of the moves and actions of the cast, having props ready when they are needed. They must work well as a team and be able to handle difficult situations and people with tact and good humour. Most acting courses include a stage management component but it is also possible to specialise. Not all courses require formal qualifications but you will have to demonstrate a high degree of intelligence at interview, as well as artistic flair, a sense of authority, an obvious enthusiasm for the theatre and some experience of backstage work.

The Stage Crew

These people require split-second timing and great physical strength to carry out their job, which includes scene-shifting, construction and set-changing (ie removing the set from the stage at the end of a run). Often entrants come from a craft background and move into the theatre when a suitable opportunity comes up.

Production Staff

Such staff are employed in most theatres but only the larger ones have different departments for armoury, metal, carpentry, paint and props. Most small theatres will employ an all-rounder to do these jobs and will quite often use other members of staff in a similar capacity.

Property Staff

These people provide all the movable items on a set – anything from an armchair to an ashtray, and must have an eye for detail. All of their contributions will be closely scrutinised by the audience.

Wardrobe, Wigs and Make-up Staff

Such staff are employed by most large theatres. Although costumes will be hired from a theatrical costumier, a few large companies will employ cutters to make their own. Staff will also be employed to fit actors and keep costumes maintained. Wardrobe staff who can alter costumes on demand with inventiveness and creativity do well. Most actors learn make-up at college but some performers will need special attention. Make-up artists take a course or are trained by cosmetic firms. Entrance qualifications

The Theatre and Performance Arts

for courses specialising in wardrobe and make-up are the same as for designers.

The Lighting Engineer

The lighting engineer designs a plan for the production and will work with a team, rigging the lights and operating them during the performance. The team will also have responsibility for related equipment, including smoke guns and pyrotechnics. The lighting engineer will be responsible for creating the right atmosphere on stage so an in-depth knowledge of lighting techniques is essential. This can be gained through experience and training, and a number of specialised courses do exist. The Association of British Theatre Technicians (ABTT) publishes a free booklet, entitled 'So You Want to Work in the Theatre' (please send a C5 SAE) and the *Directory of Drama and Theatre Courses*, which costs £5 plus 50p postage and packing. Both publications contain useful information about technical courses.

The Sound Engineer

Sound engineers provide sound cues, electronic effects and music, and solve acoustic problems. Many of those who work as sound engineers come from a broadcasting or record industry background. Again ABTT are a good source of information.

The Box Office

The box office sells and monitors tickets. Most of the work is computerised so staff must be able to get to grips with a simple computer operating process. A manager takes overall responsibility for the box office accounts and reports to the theatre manager or the house manager.

The House Manager

A house manager is responsible for looking after the theatre and supervising its day-to-day running and maintenance. He or she must make sure that the cleaning, catering and security arrangements run smoothly, and oversee everything to do with the safety and comfort of the audience. The job doesn't require stage training or special qualifications, but experience of working in the theatre, perhaps as a senior usher or assistant house manager, would be useful.

The Press Officer

The press officer makes a press and publicity plan for each production. Working well in advance of the opening night, he or she prepares press releases, arranges for actors and directors to be interviewed, invites critics to first nights, commissions photographers and sets up displays in the theatre foyer. Press officers supervise the production of posters, mailing leaflets and programmes, often working closely with a marketing officer, who will co-ordinate direct mail-shots, advertising and other promotional projects. Many press officers have a journalistic or design background and those with an arts degree and secretarial training will find their experience good preparation for this work.

The Performers

Only a few performers start off in television, radio or film. Most of them have to 'pay their dues' by completing circuits of live sets in front of critical audiences. Comics learn quickly that certain venues are guaranteed trouble and you'd better be good if you don't want to be heckled off stage. Performing live is the only training ground for live performances so a desire to get up in front of people is an absolute prerequisite for being a performer.

This doesn't mean you have to start off singing before you can talk, like a clone of Shirley Temple. You don't have to be the world's most extroverted person either. It is also a common misconception that performers head straight for the West End. Many insist on working with the community or being part of a regional touring theatre company like Hull Truck. Thankfully, anybody has the opportunity to perform, if they want to.

After the first performance there is no prescribed route for getting on. Sometimes it's down to luck and perseverance; other times it's sheer unstoppable talent; and just occasionally it might be because someone in the business wants to make you a star. What you will need is aptitude, determination and dedication.

These days it is more common to take a college course if you wish to be an actor or a dancer, but not everybody does. Singing is harder to categorise as most learning is done on the job;

The Theatre and Performance Arts

however, most classical and some jazz singers receive formal training. Some musicians learn the basics at school and go on to study formally at a school of music, while others play air guitar in their bedroom until they can afford to buy a real one with their paper-round money. Comedians can't be taught how to be funny so they must have an inbuilt ability to make people laugh. However, they can learn from the masters of stand-up comedy, just by watching how they do it, and stealing the odd joke.

Because this book cannot give in-depth coverage of the whole range of performing arts it concentrates on those for which a qualification is almost certainly necessary.

Actor

Drama courses are either accredited by the National Council for Drama Training (NCDT) or not. Taking an accredited course gives you a better chance of finding a job afterwards, mainly because Equity allows companies to take on any number of graduates of accredited courses but only a limited number of other newcomers.

Most acting courses last three years and schools award their own diplomas to pupils who successfully complete all the components. The content and emphasis of courses vary from school to school but the aim is the same: to teach students to use their voices, bodies and imaginations. Students get the chance to show what they have learnt in full-length productions which are often watched by casting directors.

Most drama schools have a minimum age limit of 18 and an upper limit of 25–30. Entry is usually by audition and interview, both of which are usually very tough. Although many schools have no specific academic requirements, some do ask for five GCSEs at Grade C or above, or two A levels. Courses begin in the autumn term and you need to apply by early spring at the latest.

Costs vary but usually begin at £5,500 a year for stage schools, to which you must add living expenses. Many professionals take a degree course at a university first and consider going to a drama school afterwards. University courses are cheaper and while you will get a local education authority (LEA) grant for a degree course, the chances of securing one for a vocational drama course at a stage school are less certain. Because grants are discretionary for stage schools, it could all come down to where you live and how much money your council has. The only way to find out for sure is to contact your LEA. If you can't get an LEA grant, the drama school itself might be able to help finance your studies. The Poor School in London teaches a part-time course, which allows students to work and study.

It might be worth contacting the Arts Council, which sometimes supports students. If you live in Scotland, the Scottish Arts Council publishes details of some of the major trusts and foundations that might be of assistance.

Some people will have secured their first jobs and equity card before they even leave drama school but if you're the average student you'll probably be taking a different route; even Kenneth Brannagh wrote 150 application letters in his final year at RADA. *The Stage* carries job adverts and a section to advertise your own talents, but the most worthwhile publication to be seen in is undoubtedly *Spotlight*, a bumper four-volume directory of actors and actresses (also available on CD-ROM). Newcomers should book space (which costs £92.50 for half a page) well before the press dates of 1 April for actresses and 1 October for actors. *Spotlight* also acts as an intermediary when a play has to be recast urgently, advising producers who is available to play a particular part. It also publishes *Contacts*, an invaluable guide to people and services in stage, television, screen and radio.

Production and Casting Report (PCR) is sent to subscribers (£20 for five weeks) every Monday. It contains detailed information about forthcoming productions, including casting and audition times. PCR also publishes *Castingdex*, *Filmlog* and *Repertory Report*. *The Casting Sheet* also brings weekly professional and up-to-date casting information and costs £16 a month. If you want to get extra work, annual membership of the British Television and Film Extras Guild (£19.95 plus 15 per cent commission on any work found) brings details of extras needed for television and film shoots all over the country.

You may wish to approach an agent, but as agents work on a commission basis (normally 10 per cent of your earnings) they only take on people who they think they can sell. Agents fix fees, ensure their clients get proper billing and represent their interests in any dispute with management. As fees go to agents first, who deduct their share before passing it on to you, it's important to employ someone you can trust. It may be flattering to be wanted but treat the whole process in a business-like fashion.

Seventy-five per cent of Equity members are unemployed at any one time. The most immediate problem, apart from boredom, frustration and depression, is likely to be lack of money. It's important to go to your local benefit office on the first day you are unemployed – otherwise you will lose money. Acting can be a bit like playing snakes and ladders but it is important to keep playing as any lack of effort will result in permanent unemployment or a career change. Although most job centres are familiar with the actor's plight, the new Job Seeker's Allowance will undoubtedly make it harder to sign on for long periods. This is because benefit offices will have discretionary rights to cut your benefit if you are offered work for which they think you are suitably qualified, and turn it down.

Any temporary work you take on needs to be something you can give up at a moment's notice, and preferably with an employer who will be sympathetic if you want time off for auditions. Temping as a secretary, writing articles and short stories for magazines and newspapers, bar work and cooking, are all popular choices. Being unemployed is a real test of how much the theatre means to you.

Dancer

There are three main dance forms: ballet, contemporary dance and modern dance. Ballet dancers start training at a very early age so they can reach the necessary levels of physical fitness and artistic brilliance. Contemporary dance is a much freer form, with the whole floor space being used and movements being much less formal. Rather more opportunities exist in the field of modern dance. Styles include jazz and tap, disco and acrobatics and work opportunities include stage musicals, television, films and cabaret.

Ideally, ballet students should attend a recognised, residential establishment such as the Royal Ballet School from the age of 11, for which there might be financial assistance. GCSEs, A levels, AS level and BTEC courses in dance do exist, but are not widely available. A few courses have been accredited by the Council for Dance Education and Training and qualified dancers find work in much the same way as actors (see above).

Working in the Media

Choreographers are usually retired dancers who have years of experience and an imaginative understanding of dance.

Dance Animateurs are employed by local authorities and regional arts authorities to initiate dance projects in schools, colleges and the local community. They must have relevant dance experience.

Musician

Most professional musicians work on a freelance basis, even if they are regular members of a large orchestra. As work isn't regular, musicians get money from recording sessions and/or teaching. Hours can be long and antisocial, with long periods of practice in between. Formal musicianship is taught in all styles, including jazz and rock, in various courses around the country. Entry requirements vary but five GCSEs are usually required, with one or more A levels being necessary for some courses. In addition, a high standard of musicianship must already have been achieved. Contact the Musicians' Union or the Incorporated Society of Musicians for more information.

The rest of the entertainment industry is made up of people who don't seek a formal education in their field. Instead, they learn by practice and performance; their numbers include comedians, children's entertainers, juggling acts, circus acts, magicians, pop, indie and rock groups, dance music DJs, many jazz musicians, media personalities, soul, blues and rap singers, and so on.

The Work Scene

Equity

Equity protects the interests of its members by insisting on the use of standard contracts that specify minimum fees and salaries and regulate conditions of employment. Because the industry is overcrowded, casting arrangements between the employers and Equity ensure that only members of Equity are eligible for work. In addition, newcomers without previous professional experience wont' be considered for the West End, television and radio, or TV commercials. So if you can't work without a card, how do you get a card?

The Theatre and Performance Arts

Every year reps, theatre-in-education and children's theatre companies can engage any number of 'registered graduates' as actors or assistant stage managers (registered graduates means they have completed an accredited drama school course). These companies are also allowed to take on a limited number of other newcomers under a quota system. Similar quotas apply for fringe companies, provincial commercial tours and pantomimes/summer seasons. Newcomers are then granted provisional membership and become entitled to full membership once they have worked for 30 weeks.

Members pay a joining fee of £35 and then an annual subscription based on their income. They include actors, cabaret artists, choreographers, circus performers, dancers, directors, designers, ice skaters, singers, stage managers, stunt performers and variety artists. For more details write to the British Actors' Equity Association.

Work in London

This comes from three main sources: commercial theatre (West End), subsidised theatre and fringe theatre. Commercial theatre has to make a profit and often relies on established stars and tried and tested formulas like the stage musical or the light comedy. Under Equity rules, newcomers can't start here. Subsidised theatre does not seek to make a profit in the same way, although it still has to balance a budget. Instead, it is supported by sponsors and not solely by ticket sales. This allows companies like the Royal Shakespeare Company to produce new plays as well as fulfilling a specified remit. The Royal Court has been called 'a writer's theatre', since it sets out to find and encourage new writing, which often has a social or political point to make. Fringe theatre is often the birthplace of radical ideas and London has a lively assortment of theatre clubs and pub theatre. With audiences often less than 100 there is an attractive, intimate atmosphere.

Work in the Regions

This also offers a number of theatrical opportunities in a whole range of different settings, from the number one touring theatres built in Victoria's reign to the many civic theatres constructed during the 1960s and early 1970s. Some perform repertory theatre and others just stage touring plays. Funding is generally low and the difficult financial conditions associated with regional theatre have led to calls for more popular fare, although some reps have managed to build up audiences with adventurous tastes. Exciting and interesting work continues to be done by the Birmingham Repertory Theatre, the Bristol Old Vic, the Chichester Festival Theatre, the Redgrave Theatre, Farnham, the Citizens' Theatre, Glasgow, the West Yorkshire Playhouse, the Royal Exchange Theatre Company, Manchester, the Liverpool Playhouse and the Nottingham Playhouse.

Alternative Theatre

Alternative theatre offers a freer artistic stance and hopes to attract audiences who don't normally go to the theatre. In fact, many performances don't take place in the theatre. Northern Broadsides performed Shakespeare in boatyards and warehouses, and others create venues from church halls, clubs, pubs, community centres and parks. Most companies are small and don't necessarily rely on props to make their point. Funding comes from regional arts boards or local authorities but many companies run on a shoestring and live in hope that some kind of backing will be forthcoming. Some of the best include Forced Entertainment, the Natural Theatre Company, Trestle Theatre, Cheek by Jowl, the Gay Sweatshop Theatre Company and the Hull Truck Theatre Company.

Community Theatre

Community Theatre seeks to work closely with local people, running workshops and devising dramatic happenings dealing with local issues. *McGillivray's Theatre Guide* has a useful list of alternative, fringe and community theatre companies.

Children's Theatre

This demands a mixture of skills, from mime and clowning to manipulating puppets, and usually involves some degree of audience participation through singing and playing games. Some take the form of workshops and encourage the children themselves to perform.

Festivals

Festivals allow a certain amount of free expression and represent a good place to try out a new act. Big ones like Glastonbury employ poets, jugglers, comedians, street performers and cabaret acts to entertain the 200,000 people who go there, and you won't need an equity card to perform. If you want to find out what everyone else is doing, this is a good place to start. Check out festival guides and find out which ones are the best for you.

Busking

This is either appreciated or hated and you can be asked to move on by the police. Most buskers are able to pursue their art without any hassles and it is a very good way of earning money while trying out your act on passing trade.

Performers offer audiences a myriad of different artistic experiences and the most interesting and appealing are often found away from closed-in theatre spaces. This chapter has concentrated on the stage because it offers more structured career openings and recognisable jobs. If you don't want to work in this way, break the mould and be original.

Performance as a Therapy

Drama Therapy

This is the intentional use of drama and theatre as a therapeutic process. It is a method of working and playing that uses action methods to facilitate creativity, imagination, learning, insight and growth. To train as a drama therapist you need a relevant first degree and a postgraduate qualification. Work comes in a number of different settings, for example, mental health clinics, prisons, private child care, and many drama therapists work on a freelance basis. For further information write to the British Association of Drama Therapists.

Music Therapy

Music therapy works along similar principles and is of great help to physically and mentally handicapped people in particular. Both music teachers and performers may work in this field and those

Working in the Media

who have completed a three-year course in music, or are experienced professional musicians, may take a one-year, full-time course in music therapy. There is also a part-time training course available. For further information write to the British Society for Music Therapy.

Courses

A number of universities and institutes of further education offer degree courses in drama and theatre arts. They are concerned mainly with drama as an academic subject. There is also an increasing number of vocational degree courses, including acting, stage management, design, wardrobe and technical arts. For further details, see *Careers in the Theatre*, Kogan Page, 1995.

Useful Addresses

Arts Council Awards: details from the Drama Officer, the Arts Council of England, 14 Great Peter Street, London SW1P 3NQ

The Arts Council of Wales, Holst House, Museum Place, Cardiff, CF1 3NX

Association of British Theatre Technicians, 47 Bermondsey Street, London SE1 3XT

British Association of Drama Therapists, 41 Broomhouse Lane, London SW6 3DP

British Society of Music Therapy, 25 Rosslyn Avenue, East Barnet, Hertfordshire EN4 8DH; 0181 368 8879

British Television and Film Extras Guild, 2nd Floor, 2–5 Old Bond Street, London W1X 3TB

British Actors' Equity Association, Guild House, Upper St Martin's Lane, London WC2H 9EJ

Conference of Drama Schools, c/o Central School of Speech and Drama, Embassy Theatre, 64 Eton Avenue, London NW3 3HY

Incorporated Society of Musicians, 10 Stratford Place, London W1N 9AE; 0171 629 4413

Musicians' Union, 60–62 Clapham Road, London SW9 0JJ; 0171 582 5566

National Council for Drama Training (NCDT), 5 Tavistock Place, London WC1H 9SS

The Scottish Arts Council, 12 Manor Place, Edinburgh EH3 7DD

Further Reading

Bloomsbury Theatre Guide, by Trevor R Griffiths and Carole Woodis, Bloomsbury, 1991

Careers in The Theatre, Jean Richardson, Kogan Page, 1995

Directory of Drama and Theatre Courses, Association of British Theatre Technicians, annual

Directory of Grant-Making Trusts, Charities Aid Foundation, annual

McGillivray's Theatre Guide, edited by David McGillivray, Conway McGillivray, annual

The Original British Theatre Directory, edited by Samantha Blair, Richmond House Publishing Co, annual

Production and Casting Report, PO Box 100, Ramsgate, Kent CT10 1UJ

Spotlight and *Contacts*, 7 Leicester Place, London WC2 7BP.

The Stage and Television Today, Stage House, 47 Bermondsey Street, London Bridge, London SE1 3XT

Chapter 4
Arts Administration, Sponsorship and Agency Work

Arts Administration

Arts administrators manage concert halls, arts centres, opera houses, theatres, touring theatre companies, orchestras, festivals, regional arts authorities, local arts organisations and the entertainment section of local councils. They work for commercial organisations, charities and local and national government.

Arts administrators will be responsible for the practical day-to-day management of an organisation. Their exact duties will depend on the type of organisation they are working for but a **theatre manager**, for example, will employ staff, book in plays, musicals, the yearly pantomime, etc and liaise with the marketing department, production department and front-of-house staff to ensure that the theatre is functioning as efficiently and profitably as possible. The job requires a certain amount of artisitic understanding in that arts administrators are generally knowledgeable about their subject and usually sympathetic to the artistic endeavours of the artists they work with. This is particularly important in a specialised field like jazz, or classical music, where margins are tight. Promoters and administrators are often first-class fundraisers and some organisations will employ people with special skills in this area. Large arts organisations will recruit education officers, audience development officers and community arts workers, all of whom help the marketing process as well as fulfilling some sort of social function.

Arts Administration, Sponsorship and Agency Work

A large organisation with a specific cultural remit, such as a national orchestra, will employ several administrators. The work will be co-ordinated by a **managing director**, who will be responsible for planning; budgeting; finding engagements by, among other things, maintaining good relations with promoters, record companies, film and broadcasting companies; and handling sponsorship. The manager is generally backed up and assisted by an **administrator**. The **concerts manager** liaises with promoters, arranges rehearsals, books halls and sees to it that conductor and players know exactly where to go and when. The **personnel manager** attends all the rehearsals and concerts and, if there is no stage manager, may be required to put out chairs, music stands and music. The work calls for knowledge of the orchestral repertoire and excellent organisational skills.

Some **promoters** become public figures, synonymous with the art form they promote; for example, Cameron Macintosh, producer of West End musicals such as CATS, or Ronnie Scott, who owned two jazz venues in London and Birmingham. Other promoters have a corporate identity like the Mean Fiddler organisation, and some just create massive festivals such as Glastonbury because they happen to have the resources (in this case, land) to do so.

The number of festivals in Britain has risen dramatically in the last few years, their unique format often seen as a way of promoting a particular area or art form which has popular or at least sustained, minority interest. Jazz, comedy, circus, juggling, rock, indie, opera, classical, folk, sea shanty, poetry and any number of other art forms all have their own festival. Few of them, however, keep their offices open all year round. The **festival director** is responsible for overall planning and for securing funding. Shortly before the festival begins, the director has to hire such people as box-office staff, ushers, stage managers and transport personnel and, when the festival is on, supervise them. Some 'wannabe' arts administrators find a stint with a festival, particularly the big one in Edinburgh, a valuable experience which helps them to convince potential employers that their passion for the arts goes beyond watching The South Bank Show.

Non-commercial (subsidised) arts work in this country is supported by a network of funding bodies, including local and county councils, but the largest patron of the arts in the UK is the Arts Council. Each major arts discipline is represented by a team of specialised officers who advise committees on the allocation of funds. There are separate councils for Scotland, Wales and Northern Ireland each one is allocated funds from central government. The funds are then redistributed to opera and ballet, contemporary music, jazz, art and photography, literary magazines, arts centres, individual artists, composers and writers. The Arts Council also supports a network of regional arts associations in England and Wales. They encourage, advise and subsidise those who promote arts events in their region.

The National Lottery has also created certain opportunities for arts specialists and fundraisers. Some regional arts associations employ personnel to advise potential applicants seeking lottery money. They must know the applications procedure and be good at filling out forms. Already, many high-profile arts projects have received lottery money.

Personal Qualities, Entry Requirements and Training

Arts administrators need to be calm and practical and possess excellent powers of organisation. They must be able to get on with all sorts of people from international performing stars to removal people, and in the early stages of their career be prepared to do practical jobs when necessary. The work calls for great attention to detail. Experience is as important as formal educational qualifications, and knowledge of the art you would like to administer is practically indispensable. Courses in arts administration include postgraduate qualifications, short, in-service training programmes and a small number of relevant first degrees. Drama students often take arts administration as an option, which is useful when combined with secretarial skills and front-of-house experience.

Getting early voluntary experience is important as employers will want you to be able to demonstrate a practical interest in arts administration. Offering your services to a local dramatic group, organising an arts event, writing reviews of local productions for a local paper or university arts magazine, producing a play for a youth group or university drama society, are all standard options. Taking part-time casual work with a local theatre is another good way of getting valuable work experience. Jobs include ushering, bar work for those aged 18 or over, leaflet distribution and box office.

Festivals have become a good focus for those interested in a particular art form. If the work isn't paid, which it often is, payment comes in the form of a free ticket to the events on offer. Find out from your local tourist information office what events happen in your area and contact the organisers well in advance of the actual event.

Sponsorship

Sponsorship (mostly of sports and arts) is widespread in the UK and increasing; you can be involved in this activity as a giver of funds, a receiver of funds or as a sponsorship consultant. Commercial, industrial and financial institutions give sums of money, often guaranteed over a period of, say, five years, to support sport and the arts in return for publicity. Sometimes this may just be a mention in the programme, but if the sponsored event is of wide public appeal, for example, a snooker championship, a concert or play in which prestigious artists/actors take part, there will be media coverage which would be worth many thousands of pounds if it were translated into advertising terms.

Sponsorship is not a philanthropic activity; it is an arrangement made by two parties for their mutual benefit and, when large undertakings are involved, both sponsor and sponsored may appoint full-time staff to handle the business. Sponsors usually consider sponsorship as a public relations activity (see Chapter 8), not advertising, and undertake it because of what it can do for the corporate image; for this reason they are unlikely to back 'controversial' arts events or get involved with sports (men/women or teams) who receive a bad press. Those seeking sponsorship, eg orchestras, theatre companies, sports organisations, teams, need money as their box-office/gate receipts, even with full houses, do not cover running costs, and they must present an attractive 'package' that will convince potential sponsors they will get value for money.

There are now a number of sponsorship consultants who can provide expert advice for both sponsor and sponsored. For example, they can act as 'marriage broker' between potentially suitable parties, tell would-be sponsors what they can realistically expect from a given outlay, and help those seeking sponsorship to present their case.

Personal Qualities, Entry Requirements and Training

Sponsorship work calls for excellent communication skills and sound financial expertise. Its practitioners usually come from a marketing or theatre administration background, perhaps previously working for a PR department. A degree in business studies or PR qualifications would be good preparation for sponsorship work.

Agency Work

Agents work through a network of professional contacts, and for this reason you will find it almost impossible to set yourself up as an agent when you are just beginning your career. You need to gain experience, to learn judgement and to make your contacts. If you are determined to go straight from school or college into agency work, you will have to try to find a clerical or personal assistant's post in a large agency and such posts are hard to come by.

The Jobs

Agents handle the business arrangements of their clients. This could include negotiating fees, finding them work (or someone who will publish or perform their work), handling their publicity, offering them professional advice and helping them to develop their careers. In return for these services, agents take a percentage (usually between 10 and 20 per cent) of their clients' earnings.

Agents live with continuous competition. Because they take a cut of their client's wages they soon lose money and credibility if they don't seize every opportunity for them. Agents must possess negotiating skills, legal expertise and, if they arrange publicity for their clients, marketing skills. Agent's clients can be 'difficult', eg sensitive, temperamental, moody or egomaniacal, so tact and patience are needed in large measure.

Job opportunities are rare as they are seldom advertised. Those vacancies that do come up are usually filled by headhunting and nepotism.

Entry requirements are informal and anyone can set up an agency which must be registered with a local authority before it can operate. Anyone applying for a clerical post will be expected to have had a good general education.

Literary Agents

Literary agents act as intermediaries between authors and publishers, film, television and radio producers and theatre managers. They find a publisher (or producer) for an author's work and negotiate the best possible deal for their client. They then handle all the author's business arrangements with the publisher, thus freeing the client from a time-consuming task. Literary agents also sell non-print media rights of books to broadcast and film companies. Literary agents are frequently very supportive of their authors: they evaluate their work, sometimes suggesting changes that might be made, come up with subjects for new works and help them in their struggles with personal, financial and creative problems.

Some agents work for publishers as scouts, seeking out new authors, manuscripts and information on books published abroad, and others do the same job for television companies. Mostly, authors approach agents with a manuscript, which the agent reads and decides whether the author and manuscript are a viable proposition.

The *Writers' and Artists' Yearbook*, published by A & C Black, is a good source of information.

Theatrical Agents

Most actors, dancers, directors and choreographers hand over the business of finding work and negotiating contracts to an agent. There are a few really big agencies with large staffs and hundreds of clients; they have different departments handling theatre, film and television contracts and are sometimes impersonal. The ones which manage the big names get to know of forthcoming productions well in advance and so have the chance to suggest some of their unknown clients for smaller parts; frequently, they have close links with management. The smaller agencies offer their clients more personal attention and often get to know them well and take pleasure in helping to shape their careers.

Theatrical agents are always on the look out for new talent and attend the end-of-course productions put on by the major drama schools. Agents not only try to find work for their clients, they negotiate their fees and contracts, ensure that they get proper billing and give them professional advice, which might occasionally involve telling them to turn down a part that could harm their image.

Agents who Handle Musicians

Concert agents look after the interests of classical musicians; they may spend quite a lot of time visiting concert promoters and opera managers at home and abroad in order to 'sell' their clients. When they arrange an engagement on tour, they negotiate contracts and fees, see that their client gets adequate billing and make hotel bookings, travel arrangements, meet the client at the airport and fend off the press. Most agents start off in established agencies. For further information contact the British Association of Concert Agents, 12 Addison Park Mansions, Addison Gardens, London W14 0BE.

There are more managerial positions in the non-classical sectors, ie pop, rock, indie, jazz, folk and so on. **Managers** often start off by handling the affairs of a group of friends, and taking a share of the band's profits. Experienced managers, who have built up contacts within the industry, scout for talent, and will take on a group that they consider has potential, shape their image for sale in a crowded market and handle all the publicity. Once an act has begun to make a name in the pop music world, a manager has to keep alive, and generate new interest in it.

Music agents deal with the 'live' interests of pop musicians, running their tours in the UK and abroad. The work calls for organisational skills as it involves booking a venue, renting trucks, renting sound and lighting equipment, erecting a stage, hiring security people and a tour manager, arranging advertising and advance publicity.

Courses

There are only a few specific arts administration courses, some of which are listed below. Many management courses enable students to combine an interest such as music with a vocational subject like business. Because the possible combinations are too endless to list here, you should read the management section of the UCAS *Official Guide*, which contains complete lists of all degree course options. Employers often consider business and secretarial qualifications useful.

Arts Administration, Sponsorship and Agency Work

Degree Level Qualifications

Arts Administration and Music Industry Management, Buckinghamshire College
Arts and Education, Bretton Hall
Arts Management, De Montfort University
Arts Practice and Cultural Policy, Coventry University
Media Production Management, West Herts College
Media Studies with Business Studies, Suffolk College of Further and Higher Education
Media with Business Management and Information Technology, University College Warrington

BTEC/SCOTVEC Qualifications

BTEC HND in Business and Finance (Broadcasting and Media Management), New College Durham
BTEC HND in Media Production with Business Studies, Farnborough College of Technology
Diploma in Television and Video Production Management, Chichester College of Arts, Science and Technology
Postgraduate Diploma and MSc in Media Management, University of Stirling
SCOTVEC HNC and Diploma in Arts Management, Fife College of Technology
SCOTVEC HND in Promotions and Events Management, Fife College of Technology

Useful Addresses and Further Reading

See pages 50–51 in Chapter 3, pages 105–6 in Chapter 8, and pages 118–19 in Chapter 9.

Chapter 5
Publishing and Printing

Book Publishing

General Publishing

Most people are familiar with general (or trade) publishing. It includes fiction and non-fiction, adult and children's books, whether sold in hard covers or paperback, available from shops or through book clubs.

The publishing process usually begins with a publisher or literary agent having an idea for a book. A suitable author is then found and commissioned to write it. Alternatively, an agent may have a manuscript with high sales potential for which he or she will organise an auction and then make a deal with the publisher whose offer is most favourable. Once a manuscript has been accepted, the publisher is responsible for transforming it into a book, and this will generally be done in consultation with the author. Except in the field of fiction, unsolicited manuscripts – those sent unrequested – form a very small part of publishers' output.

Usually a hardback edition comes first. Jackets are designed and produced by the publisher's art department or commissioned from a freelance designer; the publicity department adds a promotional statement about the book's contents, the author and, possibly, related titles. Jackets are sent overseas to agents who promote advance sales of the book and the home trade representatives show copies to wholesalers and bookshops. The process happens all over again for paperbacks, which account for about one-third of the publishing turnover in the UK.

Sometimes a special edition will be produced for book clubs. The club pays a lump sum in advance or signs a royalty-based deal from which the author receives an agreed share of the net receipts. Authors will also receive a percentage of any overseas editions, which may be purchased from the home publisher and translated for consumption abroad.

Heavily illustrated works are costly to produce and if a publisher can produce an enticing manuscript, backed up by a well-illustrated dummy of the book, he or she could persuade a consortium of overseas publishers to undertake simultaneous editions, thus greatly reducing the production costs. Some companies, known as packagers, do not publish anything but specialise in originating and producing co-editions to sell to publishers who may lack the resources to undertake such ambitious projects.

Specialist Publishing

Educational publishers provide the entire range, from first school readers to postgraduate studies. Prices must be kept low and publishers try to ensure that their titles get on the recommended reading lists. A successful textbook brings rewards for both publisher and author over many years.

Dictionaries, encyclopaedias and reference books require considerable investment by publishers as each project needs a general editor, as well as a team of sub-editors, researchers and other contributors. The editorial workload is immense and must be executed to a strict deadline. Yearbooks and directories are compiled in-house from both existing sources of information and specially commissioned questionnaires; they are produced under great pressure, as their commercial success is dependent upon the speed and accuracy of their updating.

Encyclopaedias or extended studies (on subjects such as twentieth-century warfare) may be produced in heavily illustrated magazine-format instalments, known as partworks, for monthly or weekly purchase from newsagents. The high cost of the complete work may not be apparent when each part is sold at a comparatively modest price. If the number of subscribers falls off, the publishers' costs will rise as the book has to be completed. At a later date, suitable extracts may be collected and reprinted as a hardback book.

Fine art books contain high-quality reproductions of works of art; many of them are the works of contemporary artists. By limiting such editions to a standard number, the publisher can enhance their value. Each plate may be a very fine print and sometimes a signed print will be incorporated in each copy.

Book publishers are increasingly exploiting the possibilities offered by electronic media: the conversion of books into a presentation combining text with image, sound, animation or video, or any combination of these. CD-ROM (compact disc-read-only memory) has made it possible to produce an enormous amount of mixed media on a single disc, so that whole encyclopaedias, complete with pictures and interactive components, fit on to one CD.

Jobs in Book Publishing

Publishing houses differ in their structure, but most have three main departments: editorial, production/design, and sales and marketing. Additionally, there are the service departments found in most commercial offices: accounts, reception, personnel, warehousing and distribution. Secretaries are attached to each department and sometimes move across the floor into the publishing sector.

Editorial

This is the department which attracts the most applicants, although editors are a very small percentage of the total publishing labour force. The editorial department takes the author's manuscript and, in due course, hands back a bound book. Editors liaise with those involved in the design, planning and production of each book. They read and edit the manuscript, prepare it for the typesetter, check the proofs and are responsible for assembling all the various parts, paginated in the correct order, for the printer. There is no automatic promotion system or salary structure. In a small company the only way to move up may be to move out. A degree is useful (essential in specialist academic fields), but often insufficient by itself. There is little or no formal pre-entry training and the work is usually learnt on the job. Languages are useful, and all editors should be able to type.

The Editorial Director
The editorial director has the top position and a seat on the board. In some houses there are managing editors, who combine the roles of manager and editor. They may run a centralised copy-editing department, and commission and supervise freelance editorial workers.

Acquisitions or Commissioning Editors

Also known as sponsoring editors or publishers these people are the list builders and their main task is to find authors and books of quality. They will not necessarily have worked their way up through the department but could have been engaged because of their specialist knowledge or contacts. They buy book rights, commission translations, find new authors, read and report on commissioned and unsolicited manuscripts and proposals, keep established authors happy and negotiate with literary agents. Working with the minimum of supervision they originate large projects, set up a team to carry them through and deliver the finished package within budget and on time. They must be capable of spotting and capitalising on new buying trends and markets.

Desk Editors

Also known as sub-editors or copy-editors, desk editors read a manuscript several times, check it for copyright material and prepare it for the printer. They check references and facts, correct grammar, spelling and punctuation, discuss revisions with the author, decide picture content, design and produce schedules, choose the illustrations, and draft the jacket blurb and catalogue copy. They hand the edited manuscript to the design department for production. Once the manuscript has been set in type, they send a set of proofs to the author, proof read one themselves, collate the two sets of corrections and return the proofs (via the production department) to the printer. Books with a complicated make-up usually go through several proofing stages and as the desk editor is responsible for creating a book that is good enough for publication, it is important to get it right.

Editorial Assistants

These are publishing novices. Most of them have secretarial skills and, under the guidance of a senior editor, perform basic editorial tasks, such as preparing captions for illustrations, researching bibliographical information, updating books for new editions, obtaining pictures and so on.

Paperback and Book Club Editors

These editors evaluate the suitability of works for their company's list. When the originating publisher first submits a work in manuscript they make suggestions about possible changes to the text, design or cover, which would make it more acceptable to them, and negotiate a contract. The editorial work will be carried out by the packaging publisher for the book club but paperback houses tend to originate and edit their own titles.

The Copyright and Permissions Editor
He or she deals with requests from individuals and other publishers to reproduce passages or illustrations from its copyright works.

Picture Researchers
Picture researchers are provided with a list of pictures or subjects which are needed for a book, or given a copy of the manuscript, briefed on format and design and asked to provide an agreed number of suitable pictures. Some months may be allocated for the acquisition of illustrations so researchers are usually able to work on a subject in-depth but deadlines on partworks and periodicals tend to be short. Publishing houses build up their own picture archives with which picture researchers must become familiar; they also need a knowledge of worldwide picture sources, and of copyright regulations. Picture researchers need curiosity, imagination, visual awareness and versatility, and an eye for detail. They must also be able to deal with people, as negotiation and persuasion form a large part of the job. Entry qualifications for picture editors range from GCSEs (or equivalent) to degrees, depending on the company. There is no formal pre-entry training and the work is usually learnt on the job. Experience in a library would be useful.

Production

The Production Controller
The production controller draws up an accurate specification for the book and invites tenders from typesetters, printers, paper suppliers and binders. When all the estimates have been received, the production controller places orders and ensures that all the production stages are carried out to the required standard, and on schedule. Undemanding production work on, for example, leaflets or reprints, is often given to a production assistant, who is regarded as a trainee.

The Production Director
The production director who at some stage of his or her career will have been a production controller, has a seat on the board of directors, production directors are policy makers and carry considerable financial responsibility. Usually, one of the production executives will have responsibility for the book jackets and covers, probably engaging a freelance designer to do the work.

Design

Designers
Designers prepare layouts, sketches, specimen pages and dummies and mark up the manuscripts for the typesetter after they have been edited. All the activities of the design department are managed by the design director. They discuss illustrated or complicated technical books with the author and the editor, commission freelance artwork, arrange the in-house preparation of artwork and impose a visual style on the company product. See Chapter 9 for more details.

Sales, Marketing and Publicity

Chapter 8 covers this subject in depth. Depending on the size of the company, there will be one department or three working on the promotion and selling of books. A sales director controls the activity of the department, which will involve wringing as much free publicity from the media as possible. Applicants are usually graduates, but as usual there are exceptions. Applicants should be creative, be able to write lively and informative copy, have a talent for PR and a good telephone manner.

Periodical Publishing

The organisation of magazine groups differs from that of book publishing and has much in common with newspapers (see Chapter 7 on journalism); the main areas of activity outside the service departments are editorial, advertisement sales and circulation.

Editorial

Generally speaking, competition for places is greatest in less specialised fields. As with book publishing, pre-entry training is minimal and each publishing group or individual periodical will have its own requirements.

Editors control the content of a periodical; they commission articles or visual material, write articles themselves, select suitable material from unsolicited contributions and prepare the whole for publication. The editor must have a deep knowledge of the periodical's subject matter.

Sub-editors and **editorial assistants** prepare the copy under the editor's guidance, carry out research, check facts, obtain pictures, deal with correspondence and, in some offices, do layout work.

Design

The range of work includes cover design, typographical design, layout, design of advertisements and direct mail material. Entrants will need a design qualification, details of which can be found in Chapter 9. Many magazines demand a working knowledge of a DTP (desk-top publishing) computer programme, particularly Quark Xpress.

The **art editor** places illustrations in the text, insert advertisements in the positions paid for, and gives each edition the coherence and style expected by regular readers.

Production

Production staff are trained in the printing trade. It is their responsibility to see the magazine is available at point of sale on publication day and this involves meticulous planning and a tolerance of stress.

Advertisement Sales

Commercial magazines depend on advertising revenue for survival. Graduates are often recruited straight from university to sales posts and they are trained on the job. Sales staff must know the magazine's readership and build up advantageous contacts with potential advertisers. They spend a lot of time researching, analysing and planning, and need a persuasive manner and numerical skills.

Publishing and Printing

Circulation

The circulation department must achieve maximum sales from the wholesale trade, from the team of persuasive sales representatives, through to the distribution manager, who ensures prompt delivery of the final product. The large magazine groups recruit graduates or people with A levels or equivalent if they are aged 21–24.

Allied Occupations and Freelance Opportunities

Publicists

Publicists undertake anything from a single promotion to a complete publicity campaign. They design, plan and arrange for the printing of leaflets and catalogues, organise advertising, direct mailings, review copy distribution and press cuttings, arrange authors' tours, presentations and interviews, and some will undertake print buying, sales and marketing. Companies are usually small and entry is often by recommendation.

Editorial, Literary and Production Services

Such organisations offer the entire range of publishing services to publishers, advertisers and public relations officers who need material to be written, prepared for press, researched, revised or updated. They recruit from experienced publishers by recommendation.

Indexing

Indexing is a requirement of most publishers and authors can either do the work themselves or hire a professional indexer. Most indexers gain their initial experience in publishing house editorial departments and then work freelance. The Society of Indexers administers an open-learning indexing course which comprises five units, priced £15–£20 (£20–£30 for non-members) each. As the work is freelance, payment may be by the hour (£11 being the recommended rate) or by quotation on sight of material.

Translation

Such work is often lucrative. Those considering it should read the translation section on pages 78–9.

Readers

Readers are commissioned to report on manuscripts, proposals or foreign books which are being considered for publication. They generally have publishing experience and are expected to know of rival publications which might affect a proposed book's chances of success.

Copy-editors and Proofreaders

These are often freelances. They check over manuscripts and ensure that all 'typos' and grammatical errors are corrected. Busy editorial departments will often employ proofreaders when an editor has several projects on the go at the same time.

Lexicography

This is the preparation of definitions for dictionaries or reference books. Entries for encyclopaedias and yearbooks are usually compiled by freelance writers with specialist knowledge.

Artists

Artists are employed by publishing houses, design companies, advertising firms and companies wanting their own promotional material. Some publishers take on art students during the summer vacation to do paste-up and layout work. See Chapter 9 for more details.

Printing

The purpose of printing is communication, whether the printed matter be books, magazines, newspapers, security documents or bank cards. Printers are also involved in producing wallpaper, floor coverings and even advertising slogans on milk bottles. The printing industry covers a wide range of jobs in both factory and office.

Publishing and Printing

Pre-press

Most setting is to computer floppy disc or compact disc. The operator is responsible for a keyboard, similar to that of a typewriter, which transfers typed matter for output to paper or film.

Proofreaders

Proof readers check customers' proofs for spelling mistakes and incorrect typeface before returning them. When setting to disc, proofreading is done automatically.

Camera Operators

Camera operators photograph the original of a drawing or photograph and from this produce a negative or positive as required. In colour work a separate piece of film for each colour has to be produced. The operator requires considerable skill and judgement to do this accurately. Now that the reproduction of a colour photograph is largely done by electronic scanners, not so much skill is needed on the part of the operator.

Planner/Platemaker

If not completed through computer screen, make-up planning operators take the film and place the type and illustrations in the right place in the correct pages.

Machine Minders

Machine minders set up the machines for each job, feeding in paper and plates and adjusting the inks. They then check the printed material as it comes through, making sure that the quality is consistent.

Binding and Finishing

This involves trimming the paper, assembling it into book form and pasting or stitching sheets together. In the case of hardback books the hard cover is attached (see bookbinders below).

Office Jobs

Order clerks/account executives look after individual printing jobs; they write instructions for each department and check the product's arrival into and departure from each section. Estimators work out how much a job will cost. Cost clerks go through the costs item by item and discover where and why the money was spent. Sales staff find customers, and design staff are also needed.

Bookbinders

Bookbinders produce work using centuries-old techniques with twentieth-century materials. The industry is divided between craft and mechanised bookbinding. Personal qualities include; an eye for detail; a firm but deft touch; a sense of design and a desire to produce beautiful books; and an ability to work in a production team.

Qualifications and Training

Academic qualifications are not mandatory for craft workers but the following subjects studied to GCSE level are preferred: English, maths, computer studies and science. Training, over two years, is a mixture of college placements and work on the job. To take the higher diploma in printing you will need four GCSEs and one A level or a BTEC/SCOTVEC NC/ND in printing. NVQs at levels 2 and 3 are available both for print production and print administration. In addition, there are three print-related degree courses for which two A levels are necessary. GCSEs are preferred for junior clerks and there are opportunities to gain further qualifications through BTEC/SCOTVEC or City & Guilds awards. Bookbinders need a good standard of English and arithmetic. Traineeships are offered with NVQs and there are no set time limits to completion. For more information about training, contact the British Printing Industries Federation (BPIF). Other relevant organisations include the Institute of Printing, the Scottish Print Employers Federation and the Bookbinding and Allied Trades Management Association (BATMA).

As the printing industry is changing rapidly, employees must be prepared to move with the times and retrain if necessary. As most printing involves computers, entrants should be computer literate and able to master technology quickly. A responsible attitude and a pride in what is being produced are necessary. Craftworkers need good colour vision and manual dexterity.

Courses

Publishing

Degree and **postgraduate** courses are available from: University of Brighton, Falmouth School of Art and Design, Leeds University, London College of Printing and Distributive Trades, Loughborough University, Middlesex University, Napier University, Nottingham Trent University, University of Plymouth, Reading University, Robert Gordon University, University of Stirling, Thames Valley University, West Herts College, and Wolverhampton University.

BTEC/SCOTVEC courses are available from: Falmouth School of Art and Design; Glasgow College of Building and Printing; Gloucestershire College of Arts and Technology; London College of Printing and Distributive Trades; and West Herts College.

National Vocational Qualifications are currently available in ten occupational areas: Book Editing; Editorial Management; Commissioning; Book Production; Book Design; Publicity; Book Publishing Rights; Book Publishing Contracts; Journal Management and Production Development; and Journal and Production Editing. There are no entry requirements, but 18 months' experience is recommended. Candidate registration is £150 plus VAT (level 3) and £200 plus VAT (level 4) (1996).

Short courses are available from the Book House Training Centre, Gloucestershire College of Arts and Technology (in Gloucester), Oxford Brookes University, London School of Publishing, London College of Printing and Distributive Trades, Middlesex University, Password Training, Training Matters, West Herts College, Watford and the University of Westminster.

Societies courses are arranged by the Association of Learned and Professional Society Publishers, the British Library Centre for the Book, Institute of Scientific and Technical Communicators, Oxford Publicity Partnership, Oxford Women in Publishing, Society of Freelance Editors and Proofreaders, Society of Indexers, the UK Serials Group and Women in Publishing.

Correspondence Courses are run by Chapterhouse Publishing, the National Extension College and Rapid Results College.

Careers in Publishing and Bookselling, from Kogan Page, has full descriptions of the kind of courses on offer. Alternatively write to the organisations themselves.

Printing

Printing courses at degree level are available at the London Institute, Manchester Metropolitan University, Nene College and Nottingham Trent University, West Herts College, Watford, University of Wolverhampton, University College Warrington.

For further information about other qualifications and training programmes contact:

Bookbinding and Allied Trades Management Association (BATMA), 12 Roy Road, Northwood, Middlesex HA6 1EH; 01923 821037

British Printing Industries Federation (BPIF), 11 Bedford Row, London WC1R 4DX; 0171 242 6904

Institute of Printing, 8 Lonsdale Gardens, Tunbridge Wells, Kent TN1 1NU; 01892 538118

Scottish Print Employers Federation, 48 Palmerston Place, Edinburgh EH12 5DE; 0131 220 4353

Useful Addresses

Book House Training Centre, Book House, 45 East Hill, London SW18 2QZ; 0181 874 2718/4608

London College of Printing and Distributive Trades, Elephant and Castle, London SE1 6SB; 0171 514 6500

London School of Publishing, 69 Notting Hill Gate, London W11 3SJ; 0171 221 3399

Publishers' Association, 19 Bedford Square, London WC1B 3HJ; 0171 580 6321

Society of Freelance Editors and Proofreaders, 38 Rochester Road, London NW1 9JJ; 0171 813 3113

Society of Indexers, 38 Rochester Road, London NW1 9JJ; 0171 916 7809

Society of Young Publishers, c/o J Whitaker & Sons Ltd, 12 Dyott Street, London WC1A 1DF; 0171 836 8911

Women in Publishing, Training Officer, Amanda Harting, 56 Dudley Road, Walton-on-Thames, Surrey KT12 2JU

Further Reading

The Bookseller, weekly
Careers in Journalism, Peter Medina and Allan Shepherd, Kogan Page, 1996

Careers in Publishing and Bookselling, June Lines, Kogan Page, 1996
Inside Book Publishing: A Career Builder's Guide, Giles N Clark, Blueprint, 1994
Publishers in the UK and Their Addresses, Whitaker, annual
Publishing News, 43 Museum Street, London WC1A 1LY, weekly
The Writers' and Artists' Yearbook, A & C Black, annual

Chapter 6
Writing

Introduction

'I enjoy writing, I'm quite good at it, and I'd like a career in the media. What should I do?' If your long-term aim is to become a full-time freelance writer, you should probably start by looking for a salaried job because you will need a regular income while you are building up your reputation and your contacts and finding out what the openings are. You may have gained an arts degree and then gone into some totally unrelated field, such as merchant banking or marketing, and are doing your writing in the evenings or weekends. It requires great strength of mind to make yourself sit down and write at the end of a hard day and only the most dedicated complete anything under these circumstances. However, it can be done and the satisfaction of having something accepted will keep you at it.

You may, on the other hand, have gone straight into a 'writing' job and become a trainee reporter, copywriter, public relations officer or joined an editorial department in a publishing house. Possibly an interesting career in one of these fields will open up to you, but if it does not, you will have served a useful apprenticeship and learnt how to turn out a given number of words on a given subject to a deadline.

Many people who start out as salaried employees in an advertising agency, PR consultancy or publishing house go freelance after a few years and gradually widen the scope of their writing as they discover where their interests lie. There are any number of potential markets for work of all sorts; only a very small proportion of published writing is uncommissioned so learn where the markets are, how to exploit them and plan your schedule so that you have a regular income. A writer, like an investor, should build up a portfolio of short- and long-term projects, one-off assignments and regular earners; you can obtain advice on how to do this from the Writer's Portfolio Service. You should also look into the question of getting a literary agent (see Chapter 4) to market your work for you as you can waste a great deal of time waiting to hear from publishers to whom you have sent an unsolicited (and possibly unsuitable) manuscript. Literary agents are listed in the *Writers' and Artists' Yearbook*.

The Markets

Most writers read books about writing for film, radio and television before they submit any written work and many have completed a recognised course. Chapters 1 and 2 on broadcasting, and film and video contain useful information about the various possibilities for writers. You should also consider writing to one of the film organisations mentioned in the Useful Addresses in Chapters 2; many young film directors write their own film stories as well and some industry-sponsored competitions help promote new writing work. The British Film Institute (BFI) and the Arts Council may be able to help a young writer with script ideas but it is more usual for these organisations to assist people who can already show a portfolio of previous work. Writing for broadcasting and film is a very difficult area to enter and there is no structured way of getting in.

Many television writers are already famous for their published work, for example, Colin Dexter (*Morse*), Ruth Rendall (*Wexford*), Jonathan Gash (*Lovejoy*) and James Herriot (*All Creatures Great and Small*). Some writers, such as Alan Bennet, come from a theatre background. All writers know something about their subject and many will have direct experience of it. The writers of *Dad's Army*, *Hi-De-Hi* and *It Ain't Half Hot Mum*, three of Britain's longest running situation comedies, built up a stack of comic memories by actually being in the situations they wrote about. Similarly, comedians are always conscious of how people really are. Reading and watching the great works of broadcast and film will provide you with a good education. If you don't already have a passion for viewing or listening, it would be useful to develop one.

The most successful playwrights understand their audiences well. The three most performed playwrights are William Shakespeare, Alan Ayckborn and John Godber. It is a strange coincidence that the last two are living and working within 60 miles of each other in Scarborough and Hull. Both write with a particular audience in mind. John Godber writes primarily about northern working-class culture and more generally about things people can identify with, like going to a nightclub (*Bouncers*), winning the lottery (*Lucky Sods*) and playing rugby (*Up 'n' Under*). Because of this his plays attract new audiences to theatre.

Of course, there are thousands of different theatre styles, from pantomime to rock biography to musicals, and so on. Watch lots of everything and learn from what you see. If you can't afford the high prices, you could get a job as a theatre usher; most theatres offer their staff complimentary tickets but check this first.

It is hard when you are an unknown playwright to find a producer who will put on your play but it should be easier to persuade an amateur group or provincial repertory theatre to perform your work. Many young writers cut their teeth at university, writing for their own drama department or drama society, or becoming involved in stand-up comedy evenings and reviews. Michael Palin, John Cleese and Rowan Atkinson have all followed this route. You can discover what has been produced where by reading *The Stage*, which is available through most newsagents or from the address listed on p.51. Contact the Arts Council to see what help is available.

Magazines and Newspapers

These offer the biggest potential market to the freelance writer (see Chapter 1). Editors look for a range of contributions, depending on the type of publication. Writers can earn from £5, for a published letter to a women's magazine, upwards. A survey conducted in September 1996 by *Writing Magazine* found that writers can earn £30 for a car boot sale story, £75 for the story of your operation, £150 for a 'It Happened to Me' story and £200 for amazing, true life stories.

If you don't want to contribute to a women's magazine, there are some 7,500 periodicals published in the UK so you won't have any problem finding a magazine that interests you. Before you submit any material, study the market carefully; read several issues of the publication you are thinking of approaching and try to get an idea of its style and readership etc. Not all magazines accept unsolicited material and some expect contributors to offer their work for free.

Most newspapers accept contributions from freelances and a good starting point is the local press, although demand for short pieces and rates of pay are low. Some writers contribute a regular feature on a subject on which they have a special knowledge, for example gardening.

Fiction

This is a difficult field to break into. It generates high earnings for the successful few but the sales of most first novels are numbered only in hundreds and publishers turn down thousands of unsolicited manuscripts every year. If you are to be a successful novelist, you need a burning desire to tell stories and the patience and dedication to work alone for long periods. Motivation cannot be generated artificially and most writers have a passion for books. Read extensively and make sure you keep up with the latest changes in the publishing markets (see Chapter 5). Walk round some of the larger bookshops and you will soon learn what sort of material is in demand.

If you don't want to follow the market trends, and can't find a publisher to produce your work, consider publishing the book yourself. Some books published in this way, but not many, go on to reach the bestseller list after they come to the attention of a professional publisher.

Every fiction writer hopes to earn money from selling on the subsidiary rights to their book; these could be paperback, foreign, serialisation, digest, book club and film rights.

Non-fiction

This market is more than four times the size of the fiction market and includes the lucrative educational sector. Very few unsolicited non-fiction manuscripts are published so before you start work on a non-fiction book you should interest a publisher. Write a preliminary letter and enclose a synopsis. If the publisher is at all interested, he or she will want to discuss the project with you and will very probably be able to make helpful suggestions for improvements. You should also consult the Arts Council's 'books in progress' service to find out whether anyone else is working on the same subject.

Children's Books

These include both fiction and non-fiction and publishers usually divide the readers into three age groups: the under-eights, the eights to fifteens, and young adults. Illustrations in books for younger children are as important as the text and if you can do your own you will make twice as much money, but if you cannot you will usually be consulted about the choice of artist.

Broadcasting

Broadcasting offers enormous scope, radio more than television, and with radio there is the added attraction that you may be asked to broadcast your own material if you have a good microphone manner. Television, on the other hand, pays better. You should be thoroughly familiar with the output of the station/channel/service that you would like to contribute to and it is important to submit your material to the right department. For example, BBC Radio is divided into drama, light entertainment, talks and documentaries, music, Radio 1, Radio 2, outside broadcasts and current affairs. Broadcasting organisations do not expect writers to produce only original work; sometimes they are commissioned to make adaptations of novels or short stories or to contribute to a long-running serial.

Feature Films

Such films may start life as short stories or novels and the adaptations are often made by established writers. Script writers must think visually, understand how a film is put together and be able to imagine the finished picture. If you have an idea for an original screenplay, the best way to try to market it is through an agent who specialises in film scripts. Only a minute proportion of scripts are accepted for development and very few finally get made into films. You can learn about script writing techniques at film school and script writing for television commercials provides good practice in visual story telling.

Translation

This can be divided up into two main categories: technical, scientific, commercial, eg textbooks, instruction manuals, learned articles, research findings, etc, and literary, eg novels, plays, poems, etc. The former is well paid and calls for expert knowledge of the subject. There are salaried posts for translators, work with translation agencies or self-employment. Literary translation is a difficult field to break into. Publishers pay scouts to look out for suitable foreign books and when they buy the rights on a book they commission a translation, generally from an established translator or author, or an expert in the field, eg an academic. It is not advisable to submit an unsolicited translation of a whole book to a publisher; instead, write a letter asking if you may submit an extended sample of your work. Literary translators always translate into their mother tongue, they need an excellent command of English and great awareness of style.

Editorial Work

This is covered in Chapter 5, but could include ghost writing, which is the art of turning a poorly written book (usually by a well-known personality) into something that can be sold.

Getting Started

Writing is an occupation where nothing succeeds like success; that is to say, once you have satisfactorily completed your first job others will follow. The difficult part is breaking in and when the rejection slips come you just have to try again with another publisher, periodical or broadcast organisation. All good writers have been rejected and many a publisher has failed to spot a bestseller. You can save yourself both time and anguish by observing a few elementary rules when presenting work. Your text should be typed double spaced on A4 paper; leave generous margins and use one side of the paper only. Send an SAE for the return of your manuscript. Not all publishers will read unsolicited manuscripts so it is advisable to write an exploratory letter.

Research before you submit: how long are the articles in this periodical, does that publisher like steaming sex or happily-ever-after romance, who listens to this radio network, what sort of audience go to that theatre?

The *Writers' and Artists' Yearbook* is an excellent reference source. As well as listing all the major publishing houses, periodicals and newspapers, it includes articles on the publishing trade, writing, becoming self-employed, commissioning an agent and so on. It also lists the various publications designed specifically for writers. The Writers' Guild of Great Britain is one of the recognised writing bodies and although it only lets in published writers, you should find out what services it offers. Other useful organisations are the Institute of Scientific and Technical Communicators and the Society of Authors.

Training is available from a number of sources. There are a wide range of short courses advertised in *Writing Magazine* and the *Guardian* media section on Mondays. Opinions vary about the usefulness of such courses; many people claim that writing cannot be taught, although most would agree that writing courses can teach you about markets and something about the techniques of writing for a number of different media. It is also taught as an academic subject at university, at degree and postgraduate level, sometimes as a whole subject, or as a subsidiary subject. Creative writing classes are often taught at evening class and although standards of courses vary enormously, they do provide a useful focus for activity. Whenever you are considering a course always make thorough enquiries before you enrol.

Courses

There are a few degree courses which study the creative writing process. Some of the following treat writing as a subsidiary subject so always check the university prospectuses for the exact details: Bolton Institute of Higher Education, Bournemouth University, Dartington College of Arts, University of Derby, University of East Anglia, Gwent College of Higher Education, Liverpool John Moores University, Manchester Metropolitan University, Middlesex University, Norwich School of Art and Design and Rose Bruford College.

Useful Addresses

Institute of Scientific and Technical Communicators, Kings Court, 2–16 Goodge Street, London W1P 1FF; 0171 436 4425

Society of Authors, 84 Drayton Gardens, London SW10 9SB; 0171 373 6642

The Writers' Guild of Great Britain, 430 Edgware Road, London W2 1EH; 0171 723 8074 (published writers only)

The Writers' Portfolio Service, 51 Washington Road, Maldon, Essex CM9 6BN

Further Reading

Many of the books listed at the end of Chapters 2, 5 and 7 are aimed at writers.

Willing's Press Guide, British Media Publications, annual
Writers' and Artists' Yearbook, A & C Black, annual. Details of publications and payments are printed, and names of the relevant editors are listed
The Writers' Handbook, Macmillan, annual
Writing Magazine, Writers' News Ltd

Chapter 7
Journalism

Introduction

It is possible to become a journalist without training but you are more likely to get the job you want if you have one of the recognised qualifications (details of which appear in the following pages). Although a course will teach you the technicalities of your craft, most trainee journalists already have a good command of English and can relate to the idea of news. If you aren't interested in news or the communication of information through journalism, no amount of practical training will bring the enthusiasm you need to survive and do well in this highly competitive and often stressful industry.

Working for Newspapers

Most start their career by completing a training contract or a period of indentured employment at a small local provincial paper. From there it is possible to move to one of the larger provincial papers and eventually to the nationals, or into radio and television. Starting with a local newspaper is an excellent beginning as you encounter the whole range of stories a newspaper has to cover, from day-to-day events such as weddings, funerals, court cases and local council reports, to the more unusual stories such as fires, anti-road protests and royal visits. Trainee reporters learn essential techniques, including shorthand, journalism law, sub-editing, layout and caption writing.

Training for Newspaper Journalism

Training for newspaper journalism is compulsory and all trainee journalists must reach the recognised standard set by the National Council for the Training of Journalists (NCTJ). It is available directly from employers as on-the-job training, or from colleges. Direct-entry training is supplied by local and provincial papers, who either follow a scheme administered by the NCTJ or operate their own individual training programmes. Large publishing companies tend to have their own programmes because they recruit large numbers of applicants every year. Details of these should be obtained directly from the companies involved. All training programmes combine on-the-job training with some classroom work and usually lead to a NVQ level 4 qualification in Journalism.

Entrants following the NCTJ programme normally serve a six-month trial period before being accepted as trainees. After that, a distance-learning pack must be completed before the final training stage, a 12-week, college-based course, commences.

Students with A levels or a degree can take a pre-entry, one-year, full-time vocational course at one of the colleges accredited by the NCTJ. This skips the direct-entry training process and allows students to study wholly in a college environment before embarking on their career. All training routes include the teaching of essential subjects such as journalism law, public affairs and shorthand.

Press Photography

Twenty trainee photographers are recruited to the industry each year. Minimum educational qualifications required for acceptance on to an NCTJ training scheme are the same as those for reporters (see below). If you don't have the required number of GCSE passes, you can still do the course if you've got two years' relevant experience or an equivalent qualification in photography.

Training takes place on the job and in two eight-week block release courses held at Stradbroke College in Sheffield. Again, an NVQ level 4 in Newspaper Journalism (press photography) is available. Alternatively, you can take a pre-entry course in press photography or photojournalism, again at Stradbroke.

Cost of Training

Direct entrants have their training paid for by their employer, and will also receive a salary. Trainees on a pre-entry course might get funding from their local education authority (LEA) but this is by no means certain. A free copy of *Student Grants and Loans: A Brief Guide* should be available at your local job centre or careers office.

Postgraduate pre-entry courses can cost between £500 and £2,750, and you'll have to find money to live on as well. This isn't easy and your LEA is unlikely to offer funding. The Department for Education and Employment makes interest-free Career Development Loans which you must start paying back within the first year of employment; phone 0600 585 505 for details.

Getting Started

The NCTJ publishes a useful leaflet entitled *A World of Challenge*. It contains a list of accredited colleges, in-company training schemes and access courses for those who don't have the necessary GCSE qualifications to get a place on a pre-entry course. If you want to enter the newspaper trade directly, ask your library to order copies of *Benn's UK Media Directory* and *Willing's Press Guide*. These books contain information about British publications and a complete list of newspapers, editors and contact points within the industry. Before writing to newspapers, choose ones which will suit you. Considerations may include location, circulation, editorial style and content, and so on. Write to the editor listed in the book and ask about training opportunities, making them aware of your enthusiasm. Newspaper editors like to hear from people who know something about the paper they wish to work for so bear this in mind when writing.

Editors are impressed by people who can demonstrate the following: an interest in current affairs, people, places and events; an ability to write in a style which is easy to understand; good spelling, grammar and punctuation; a willingness to accept irregular hours; an ability to work under pressure; an appreciation of the part a local newspaper plays in the community; and a certain amount of determination and persistence.

If you decide to study for A levels or a degree, take advantage of the time you have at college to get some more experience. Writing for a college newspaper, making up your own newsletter, sending letters to the local paper, writing up reviews of local events, even carrying out a work-experience placement, all help editors to notice your application in the stacks they receive.

Qualifications Needed

Trainee Reporters

Five GCSE passes (grades A to C) or equivalent; or one A level or two AS level passes, plus four GCSE passes or equivalent in different subjects; or two A level or four AS level passes, plus two GCSE passes or equivalent in different subjects.

One-year Full-time Pre-entry Course

Two A level or four AS level passes (grades A to C) or equivalent; one A level or GCSE pass must be in English; or candidates must have completed an NCTJ-recognised access course.

Scotland

At least three Highers, including English, plus at least two Standard or O grades at levels 1, 2 or 3, in different subjects.

Over half the entrants to newspaper journalism are university graduates.

Working for Magazines

In total, there are 6,000 periodicals published in Britain. In addition to the familiar consumer magazines, there are in-house magazines distributed to members of staff, professional publications for doctors, architects, lawyers and so on, trade magazines for grocers, games retailers, caterers, etc, and magazines produced by or for organisations and associations which are either sold on subscription or supplied as part of a membership package, for example, a fan club magazine.

As well as moving between publications, it is possible to move up the career ladder by becoming a sub-editor, features editor or editor (see Chapter 5). Alternatively, you may want to become a freelance journalist, using your contacts to get work from commissioning editors. Generally speaking, only experienced journalists go freelance because work is rarely constant. Occasionally, freelance writers get their first full-time staff job by applying for a job with a magazine they already contribute to as a freelance writer.

Magazine Training

Journalists working for periodicals do not follow a compulsory training scheme like newspaper reporters. Instead they can choose from a variety of course options, some of which are recognised by the Periodicals Training Council (PTC) as being of particular value. The PTC advises that both school-leavers and graduates should take a pre-entry course, but it isn't necessary to have this sort of qualification to get a job. Some magazines will ask only that their employees have an ability to write good copy. Others will take on people for their specialist knowledge of a particular subject.

It is also possible to receive on-the-job training by joining one of the big magazine publishers. For example, Morgan-Grampian's Editorial Trainee Scheme lasts for ten months and includes periods of work on two or three different publications, along with courses in keyboard skills, shorthand, news and feature writing, interview techniques and journalism law.

All students considering taking a pre-entry course, or signing up for an indentured training programme with a publishing company, should contact the PTC and ask for a copy of their booklet, *Periodical Training*. Competition for all magazine jobs is quite tough and 85 per cent of entrants are graduates or postgraduates, many of whom have already gained valuable experience working on a student newspaper or arts magazine, either as a contributor or as an editor.

Finding out about publications is fairly easy. *Benn's UK Media Directory*, *Willing's Press Guide*, the *Writers' and Artists' Yearbook* and *The Writers' Handbook* all contain details of magazines, including the names of editors. If you want to make freelance contributions, be sure to know your market. Editors prefer to receive letters from people who are genuinely interested in the subject they specialise in. Don't be put off by rejection letters. If you enclose an SAE, you almost always get a reply and you may get one that's encouraging.

Radio and Television Journalism

At present there are probably fewer than 5,000 full-time broadcast journalists in the UK. Most start off working for a local radio station where they cover the vast majority of possible jobs. Unlike news reporters, almost all radio journalists take a postgraduate pre-entry course. It is therefore becoming increasingly desirable to have a degree, preferably in a related subject like politics, history or economics. Some journalists still make the transition to broadcasting from newspapers but the numbers are becoming increasingly rare.

Reporting from the front line in Bosnia would be considered the pinnacle of any journalist's career. Broadcast journalists learn the necessary skills to relate news, live, on the spot, and without any time to consider the framing of the actual words, whether they are reporting from a war zone in the Balkans or a by-election in Finchley. They also learn how to read the news, interview people from all walks of life and create edited features from prerecorded stories. The job is stressful and the deadlines are set hour by hour.

Training for Television

Students are quite often trained as bi-media journalists, enabling them to work in both radio and television. The accepted training route is a one-year postgraduate course from a college recognised by the National Council for the Training of Broadcast Journalists (NCTBJ). Most courses will concentrate on teaching radio journalism but they should all have components on television work.

The BBC runs two training schemes for journalists, the Regional News Trainee Scheme and the Local Radio Trainee Reporter Scheme. There are usually 1,500 applicants for the 38 places available so be prepared to put a lot of work into your application, which will have to include a recorded piece of work. Training is very good once you get in and includes a three-month study programme in London or Bristol. Here trainees learn about interviewing techniques, news collection and selection, tape-editing, writing for local radio, law and public administration, shorthand and typing.

Skillset, the industry training organisation, provides careers information for applicants wishing to work with independent companies. Most regional news programmes recruit locally known journalists with a background in radio. ITN recruits its journalists from the regional television companies. There may also be limited opportunities for experienced journalists with Sky News, or one of the cable companies.

Working in the Media

Getting Started

Undergraduates have a better chance than most when it comes to getting real radio experience, either by choosing a course that includes radio and television as component parts, or by choosing a university with a radio station. Hospital radio and community radio stations (some of which only broadcast for one month) will also allow you the opportunity to gain valuable work experience. As part of their application procedures, colleges offering postgraduate courses ask for a recorded news story of your own making so access to a studio, recording facilities and editing equipment is very useful.

All postgraduate courses include work experience placements at a local radio station. Here you will meet, and hopefully impress, potential employers. Many people get their first job in broadcasting by making a good impression in their placement week. Adverts for jobs appear in the *Guardian* on Saturdays and Mondays, in the *UK Press Gazette*, on *Ceefax* and occasionally in local papers.

Other Opportunities

Press agencies like Reuters provide a reporting service, press cuttings and photographs for newspapers and broadcasting organisations; they employ journalists and feature writers. Press agencies provide employees with indentured training in the same way as newspapers.

Government Press Service (GPS) journalists working for the GPS explain government policy and actions to the general public. They act as public relations officers, organising opportunities for ministers to publicise their work. They do not work for a political party but are employed as civil servants, who are regarded as impartial. Sometimes these jobs are advertised but you can apply at any time through a government organisation called Recruitment and Assessment Services. For careers information you should write to the Government Information Service (GIS).

Press officers are appointed by local councils, statutory authorities, arts organisations, charities, commercial and industrial firms, trades unions and so on. They almost certainly have some sort of journalistic training and, at the very least, know how to get press coverage for an event, product or service. They must be well organised, well versed in their organisation's objectives and happy to talk to the media. A journalistic background helps them understand what makes a good story.

Public relations is an occupation commonly taken up by journalists. Turn to Chapter 8 if you would like to know more.

Freelance journalists usually make the transition from full-time employment when they have more good reasons than bad for going it alone. Freelances must be confident that they will be able to secure work from a variety of sources, often from people whom they already know. More common in magazine journalism and photojournalism than newspaper or broadcast journalism, freelances don't need any particular educational qualifications and some don't come from a newspaper background. Because the market for written work is so demanding and vast, it is possible to get into freelance work from a variety of different backgrounds. Knowledge of English usage and an ability to write interesting copy and deliver it on time are, of course, essential, as is the ability to type.

Courses

Newspaper Journalism

National Council for the Training of Journalists
Accredited Courses

Three-year full-time degree course, Bournemouth University, University of Central Lancashire, City University (Graduate Centre for Journalism), Napier University of Edinburgh, Surrey Institute of Art and Design.

One-year full-time pre-entry courses in England, Wales and Northern Ireland, University of Central Lancashire, City University, Cornwall College, Darlington, Harlow College, Highbury College, Lambeth College (for ethnic minorities only), Napier University of Edinburgh, Sheffield College (Stradbroke), Strathclyde University.

Two-year HND course, Harlow College, Surrey College of Art & Design

Two-year SCOTVEC HND course, Bell College of Technology, Napier University of Edinburgh

Working in the Media

Application forms and further details are available from the NCTJ (enclose 9" by 4" SAE).

One-year postgraduate diploma courses in journalism, City of Liverpool Community College, University of Central Lancashire, City University, Glasgow Caledonian University, Strathclyde University, University of Wales College of Cardiff

18-week graduate courses are run by the NCTJ at Cornwall College and Sheffield College (Stradbroke)

Post-entry 12-week block-release courses, Darlington College of Technology, Harlow College, Highbury College, Napier University of Edinburgh, Sheffield College (Stradbroke)

Post-entry day-release schemes, Calderdale College, City of Liverpool Community College, Yale College (Wrexham Further Education Centre)

Direct-entry Training
NCTJ-accredited in-company training schemes are run by:

Croydon Advertiser Series, Advertiser House, Brighton Road, South Croydon, Surrey CR2 6UB; 0181 668 4111

Kent & Sussex Courier, Longfield Road, North Farm Industrial Estate, Tunbridge Wells, Kent TN2 3HL; 01892 526262

Midland News Association, Rock House, Old Hill, Tettenhall, Wolverhampton WV6 8QB; 01902 313131

Southern Newspapers plc, The Fountain, 1 High Street, Christchurch, Dorset BH23 1AE; 01202 480180

Trinity Newspapers, Trinity House, 51 London Road, Reigate, Surrey RH2 9PR; 0181 661 2221

United Provincial Newspapers, PO Box 168, Wellington Street, Leeds LS1 1RF; 0113 243 2701

Press Photography

One-year full-time pre-entry course, Sheffield College (Stradbroke). This is accredited by the NCTJ, who also supply application forms on demand.

One-year Postgraduate Diploma in Photojournalism, London College of Printing and Distributive Trades.

Journalism

Magazine and Periodical Journalism

One-year postgraduate course, City University, University of Wales College of Cardiff
One-year course in Magazine Journalism, Highbury College
One-year Diploma in Periodical Journalism (for ethnic minorities), Highbury College
15-week course in Training for Magazine Journalism, Journalism Training Centre
Nine-week Postgraduate Course in Magazine Journalism, PMA Training, London
Three-year BA Hons Fashion Journalism, Design and Promotion, London College of Fashion

Company training programmes are operated by Reed Business Publishing, Morgan-Grampian, IPC, EMAP and Haymarket.
Short courses are mainly organised in association with the Periodicals Training Council (PTC). For a full list, ask for the *Magazine Training Directory*.

Broadcast Journalism

NCTBJ-recognised Courses
One-year full-time postgraduate, University of Central Lancashire, City University, Darlington College of Technology, Falmouth School of Art & Design, Highbury College of Technology, London College of Printing and Distributive Trades, Trinity and All Saints College, University of Wales College of Cardiff
Intensive 25-week postgraduate summer course, University of Central England in Birmingham
Postgraduate Diploma, Broadcast Journalism, Trinity and All Saints College
Two-year HND, Print and Broadcast Journalism/BA Hons Journalism, West Surrey College of Art and Design

Other Courses

BA Hons in TV and Broadcast Journalism, De Montfort University
BA Broadcast Journalism, Nottingham Trent University

Working in the Media

BA Multimedia Journalism, Bournemouth University

BBC

Regional News Trainee Scheme for Graduates
Local Radio Trainee Reporter Scheme
Applications should be made to BBC Corporate Recruitment Services

ITV

Regional programme companies should be contacted directly for details of their formal trainee programmes which normally start in September. The ITV Network Centre runs short training courses in journalism but priority for these courses is given to ITV staff members. A minimum of six months' experience in newspaper, radio or television journalism is normally required. Subjects are varied and funding may be available from the Freelance Training Fund. For details contact the Training Department of the Independent Television Network Centre.

Useful Addresses

Press Agencies

Associated Press, 12 Norwich Street, London EC4A 1EJ; 0171 353 1515
Central Press Features, Unit 20, Spectrum House, 32–34 Gordon House Road, London NW5 1LP; 0171 284 1433
National News Agency, 30 St John's Lane, London EC1M 4BJ; 0171 490 7700
Press Association, 85 Fleet Street, London EC4P 4BE; 0171 353 7440
Reuters plc, 85 Fleet Street, London EC4Y 4DY; 0171 250 1122
United Press International, 2 Greenwich View Place, Millharbour, London E14 9NN; 0171 333 0999

Association of Independent Radio Companies Ltd, Radio House, 46 Westbourne Grove, London W2 5SH; 0171 727 2646
BBC Corporate Recruitment Services, PO Box 7000, London W5 2PA

Journalism

Bureau of Freelance Photographers, Focus House, 497 Green Lanes, London N13 4BP; 0181 882 3315

Chartered Institute of Journalists, 2 Dock Offices, Surrey Quays Road, London SE16 2XL; 0171 252 1187

EMAP Training, 57 Priestgate, Peterborough PE1 1JW; 01733 892444

Government Information Service (GIS), Marketing, Recruitment and Training Division, Information Officer Management Unit, Cabinet Office (OPSS), Horse Guards Road, London SW1P 3AL

Haymarket Publishing Group Ltd, 30 Lancaster Gate, London W2 3LP; 0181 943 5000

Independent Radio News, 1 Euston Centre, London NW1 3JG; 0171 388 4558

Independent Television Network Centre, 200 Gray's Inn Road, London WC1X 8HF; 0171 843 8077

IPC Magazines, Training and Development Department, King's Reach Tower, Stamford Street, London SE1 9LS; 0171 261 5000

Morgan-Grampian plc, The Training Manager, Calderwood Street, London SE18 6QH; 0181 855 7777

National Council for the Training of Broadcast Journalists (NCTBJ), c/o Field House, Kinoulton, Nottingham NG12 3EH; 0115 945 5119

National Council for the Training of Journalists (NCTJ), Latton Bush Centre, Southern Way, Harlow, Essex CM18 7BL; 01279 430009

National Union of Journalists, Acorn House, 314-320 Gray's Inn Road, London WC1X 8DP; 0171 278 7916

The Periodicals Training Council (PTC), Imperial House, 15–19 Kingsway, London WC2B 6UN; 0171 836 8798

Pitman Training Ltd, 154 Southampton Row, London WC1B 5AX; 0171 837 4522

Reed Business Publishing Group (Training), Quadrant House, The Quadrant, Sutton, Surrey SM2 5AS; 0181 652 8032

Skillset, 124 Horseferry Road, London SW1P 2TX; 0171 306 8585

Thomson Regional Newspapers, Editorial Training Centre, Thomson House, Groat Market, Newcastle upon Tyne NE1 1ED; 0191 201 6043

Westminster Press Training Centre, Hanover House, Marine Court, St Leonards-on-Sea, East Sussex TN38 0DX; 01424 435991

Further Reading

Please see also p.81
Benn's UK Media Directory, Benn, annual
Broadcast, weekly
Careers in Journalism, Peter Medina and Allan Shepherd, Kogan Page
Careers in Television and Radio, Kogan Page
Magazine Training Directory, PTC, annual
UK Press Gazette, EMAP Business Communications Ltd
Working on a Newspaper, Wayland
A World of Challenge, NCTJ, annual

Chapter 8
Marketing, Advertising and Public Relations

Introduction

Marketing was the big success story of the 1980s and, despite the recession, still offers a wide variety of stimulating opportunities for those interested in communication. It is generally regarded as an attitude or a way of thinking, shaping the way entrepreneurs do business by making the identification and satisfaction of customer needs a top priority. Because of this it adapts well to any organisation, big or small.

This chapter looks at marketing, advertising and public relations separately because, while a smaller organisation may have one marketing person to carry out all these activities, larger ones have specific people for each role.

A company has two choices when it comes to marketing its products. It can conduct the process from within the company by creating its own marketing department, or it can hire in a specialist agency to do the job. Often a large company will employ some marketing personnel, and buy in out-of-house specialists in areas like advertising and public relations. The work and qualifications discussed in this chapter apply equally to in-house marketing departments and out-of-house agencies.

The greatest difference between the two is probably that in-house marketing departments are working towards a common corporate goal, whereas agencies could be working on several different accounts (for different clients) at the same time, each as important as the next.

Marketing

The role of marketing is to work out what people want or will buy, making sure that the product is right for these people, and then making sure that it is available at the right price in the right places. Basically, this means taking steps to ensure that a product sells.

The structure and responsibilities of a marketing department within an organisation will vary according to the organisation's size and the importance it places on marketing, but the focus of any large marketing department is the marketing director, who has overall responsibility for the promotional activities of the company. The marketing director decides a promotional strategy for any given product, employs the necessary out-of-house agencies and co-ordinates the activities of in-house members of staff. Each department will have its own responsibilities and it will be the marketing boss who makes sure all the activities proceed at the right speed and come together at the appointed time. Take this example:

Fizz Inc wishes to launch a new soft drink in an already crowded market.

The **marketing manager** 'briefs' a **market research agency** to find out as much as possible about the market. The agency may use a combination of statistics and reports that are already available and tailor made research aimed at collecting more specific information. It provides a detailed report.

The **research and development department**, in close contact with the marketing manager, looks closely at the findings of the report and sets to work creating the new drink. After 12 months the drink is ready and the marketing manager holds a 'brainstorm' to decide the all-important name, and a selection of possibles is fed through the market research system once again. Arcadian Spring is born! At the same time packaging designs are also investigated.

The marketing manager then chooses an **advertising agency**, possibly by putting the account out to tender, and the successful agency works closely with the marketing department to plan the launch campaign. During the launch, the retailers will need to be convinced, as well as the customers.

The **sales team** is offered glossy promotional material, sales targets with prizes for those who reach their top sales figures, and an impressive presentation at the annual sales conference. The retailers are provided with free 'point of sale' display material, sales promotion incentives to stock the new drink and an impressive presentation by the sales team to persuade them to buy large stocks for the launch. Retailers also need to know how the new product will be supported by advertising and sales promotional activities.

The consumers are going to be bombarded with advertising about Arcadian Spring as the advertising agency has produced a series of television advertisements. There will also be full-page colour advertisements in women's magazines and Sunday colour supplements. At the same time the **public relations agency** used by Fizz Inc has organised a press launch, with a leading sports personality and health promoter as guest speaker. Press releases and samples have been distributed. If sales begin to flag after a successful launch, new promotions could be devised to encourage them – perhaps 'money off' vouchers.

The marketing manager has been the co-ordinator of all this activity. The planning process is critically important: many of the activities described briefly above take months to prepare. 'Marketing and Sales' are often grouped together and it is important to consider sales as part of the marketing process, especially in career terms, as many marketing training programmes ask their trainees to spend time 'at the sharp end'. In this example, the sales manager will liaise with the marketing manager at all stages of the marketing process, providing useful, first-hand experience of the customer.

What Kind of People Work in Marketing?

Regular hours and a routine day are definitely not on the cards. You will be expected to have an all-round understanding of how the business operates since you deal closely with most other departments. Your work is central to most of the company's activities and, as well as needing creative and interpersonal skills, you will need to analyse and use large quantities of financial and market research information. In addition, you will need to work well under pressure, plan in a structured way while still thinking creatively and taking advantage of all opportunities, and understand consumer needs which might be entirely different to your own.

Advertising

All advertisements offer information, but may also encourage an action – often the purchase of a product or service. An advertisement can have various objectives: to establish, maintain or enhance a company's overall image; to increase demand for a type of product or service; to increase sales of a particular product or service; to inform the public (about a hazard around the home, for example); to tell customers about a brand-new product.

An advertising agency, using a combination of people with specific skills, looks at a product or service, identifies its most desirable and believable benefits, and devises a campaign to communicate them to the target audience. Some agencies specialise in, for example, direct marketing. Others offer a more complete range of services, which would include sales promotions and public relations.

The Account Manager

He or she is responsible for the overall running of the account (the contract with the client). Taking a brief from the client, explaining it to the agency team working on the account and ensuring that the team meets a specified deadline, the account manager must be sensitive to the needs of the client at all times.

Copywriters

Copywriters think up slogans, voice-overs and any wording that will go to make up the advertisement. While copywriting is a skill that can be improved with practice and training, good copywriters have a 'knack' for finding that clever, arresting phrase and for 'hitting the nail on the head'. Just think of 'Naughty but nice', the old advertising slogan for fresh cream cakes.

Art Directors

Art directors may begin their careers as graphic artists or designers (see Chapter 9). In the agency, they will need to be able to translate a concept quickly into a visual image (to see whether it would work), and then to work that up into more detail, sometimes creating a 'storyboard' cartoon strip to demonstrate their thoughts.

Agency Producers

These people are responsible for the production of a television or film advertisement; working with an outside film company the agency producer will co-ordinate all the production personnel, location, choice of director and so on. As the agency is working as an intermediary between a client and the film crew, the producer has to ensure that the client is getting a good deal.

The Media Planner

A media planner books advertising space across the range of media available. He or she will have magazine and newspaper circulation figures and readership profiles, viewer and listener figures and profiles for television and radio programmes, and will draw up a media plan matching prospects with media within the budget and creative constraints of the campaign.

What Kind of People Work in Advertising?

If you are an avid analyser of advertisements, approach tasks creatively and enjoy the gentle art of persuasion, advertising might be the profession for you. Each advertising agency is different and demands different types of people. While a large agency might have a well-structured workforce with plenty of administrative support, a smaller company might expect to employ all-rounders who could be closely involved in most stages of a campaign. If you are interested in pursuing a career in advertising, take out a subscription to *Campaign* or *Marketing Week*, and read as much as you can about advertising techniques and the history of advertising.

Public Relations

What is Public Relations?

According to the Institute of Public Relations, 'public relations is the deliberate, planned and sustained effort to establish and maintain mutual understanding between an organisation and its public'. Nearly every organisation wants to influence the ways in which it is seen by other individuals and groups, and its 'public' can include the local community, shareholders, the employees within the organisation, the retail trade and so on.

Some public relations professionals work in-house and some work for agencies. It is also possible to work freelance, although only after having developed a strong base of contacts. In each case, the job demands close liaison with all the marketing staff within an organisation, with a clear idea of their objectives and plans. An agency will appoint account managers for each client and, as with an advertising agency, the account manager executes the communications activities for the client within the budget that has been agreed. Much public relations work involves communicating with the press, so an understanding of how journalists work is important.

Some of the most important PR activity is related to the communication of information to the general public after a disaster. This has been called 'crisis PR', and although it does not alleviate suffering, it can certainly restore confidence in an organisation much faster than if the organisation shrugs off the public in its hour of need.

What Kind of People Work in Public Relations?

Some people move from journalism to work in public relations. They understand what the press will be interested by and can present a story in the most effective way in order to get the desired coverage (or to avoid getting negative coverage). The ability to write well is essential, to pick out salient facts and express them in the most succinct and eye-catching way.

A good starting point is as a junior in an agency, or as an information assistant in an organisation. Mostly, employers wishing to fill senior positions will want people with solid journalistic or public relations experience.

Getting Started

At a time when many organisations have cut down on the number of new staff they recruit, you may find it easier to get some work experience if you can afford to work for nothing for a while. Write off to companies you have highlighted as being of interest and offer your services free in an administrative capacity for a few weeks. Make sure you have a skill to offer: good typing, wordprocessing and desk-top publishing skills are the norm nowadays. Set up the ground rules before you start and don't hang around

Marketing, Advertising and Public Relations

beyond the time deadline you have set, unless of course you can afford not to be paid for the skills you are offering. Volunteering only works if you have set goals and a specified time scale within which to work.

Job advertisements appear in the *Guardian* on Mondays and Saturdays, and in *Campaign*, *Marketing Week*, *Media Week*, *PR Week*, the *UK Press Gazette* and *Marketing*. These should all be available in a good reference library. In a similar vein, the following publications contain details of companies which may be interested in receiving speculative letters and CVs: *The Advertiser's Annual* (Reed Information Service), *BRAD Advertiser and Agency List* (EMAP), *The Creative Handbook* (Reed Information Service), *Hollis Press and Public Relations Annual*, *The Institute of Public Relations Handbook* (Kogan Page), *The Marketing Manager's Handbook* (AP Information Services). It may be worth researching the top 30 companies you would most like to work for and writing to them. Remember local organisations; look in the Yellow Pages and similar reference publications.

Traineeships are possible, and while places for these are heavily oversubscribed and preference is often shown to graduates, it is well worth finding out who offers what. Consult the relevant association to find out what's on offer and read the annual *Directory of Graduate Opportunities, GO*, published by Newpoint. See also the many annual or more frequently published careers advice and vacancy information publications.

The Institute of Public Relations and the Institute of Practitioners in Advertising (IPA) both offer a wide range of advice sheets for those seeking jobs or work experience. The IPA publishes a *Factfile* which lists the 50 or so agencies which run structured training schemes. It is only available between October and February and all inquiries must be accompanied with a large SAE.

Some people move upwards from the sales team. Sales can be tough work and usually offers a low basic salary which can be topped up by commission sales. Despite the obvious pitfalls, a job in sales cannot only get you into a media environment, but will also teach you invaluable skills as well.

When considering making an application for work experience or an advertised position, make yourself aware of the work the organisation is doing. At interview stage they are likely to ask you what you thought of some of their recent work, and about the work of other organisations. You must be aware of the state of the industry and be able to comment on current practices and techniques. If you have examples of your work, send them in. If you are going for a design job, you will need a smart portfolio with a limited number of strong pieces presented in a way that demonstrates an understanding of what that company is looking for. (Designers should read Chapter 9 as this contains useful information about qualifications and further career opportunities.)

Qualifications

People go into marketing, advertising and public relations careers with first-class degrees in history, Pitman typing qualifications, doctorates, A levels, HNDs in design, sandwich degrees in business, and a variety of other acceptable qualifications. Everyone agrees that it is you as a person, plus your experience, that counts, so although it is possible to work your way up from the bottom, recruiters have worked out that the 'raw' person they are looking for is likely to be educated to graduate level. Once you have your degree you may wish to continue with professional qualifications awarded by the institutes which govern marketing, advertising and PR.

If you don't have a degree and are unlikely to get one, there are other routes into the business, such as starting off as a secretary or as an administrative assistant. This route will undoubtedly be a hard slog because you are competing against people who are considered to be more ideal for the position. It is also possible to become a Modern Apprentice in Information Technology or Business Administration and work towards the City & Guilds of London Institute (C&G) marketing course at NVQ levels 2 and 3. Your local Training and Enterprise Council (TEC) or Local Enterprise Council (LEC) in Scotland will help you look for a suitable vacancy.

Which Degree Course?

A business related qualification at HND or degree level can show employers that you had an early commitment to business ideals and will demonstrate that you already possess an understanding of business practice and technique; a year spent in a commercial environment is often part and parcel of a degree qualification. Degree courses offering marketing, advertising or other appropriate content will make your studies even more specific and employers do like to see students who have already spent a year working in a professional environment. Yet the qualification in itself is not everything, and if it means dropping a favourite subject, you need to ask yourself, is it worth it? Some people regret missing out on the chance to study a non-vocational subject at university and others regret not having the foresight to see that a vocational course would make life easier for them when they left. Maybe it's a case of the grass is always greener.

BTEC/SCOTVEC Higher National Certificate and Diploma qualifications offer a wide range of vocational options, covering every aspect of business and office work. The Certificate and Diploma courses are on the same academic level but the Diploma covers a wider range of topics and gives more emphasis to management skills. They both generally take two years to complete, the Certificate being part time. The Diploma is equivalent to a pass degree, which is not considered to be as high a standard as an honours degree. Some people would prefer to follow a part-time or distance-learning course, especially if they have other responsibilities to consider. These are widely available and represent a good option in certain circumstances.

Professional qualifications are offered by the Chartered Institute of Marketing (CIM) and the Communication, Advertising and Marketing Education Foundation (CAM). CIM offers three levels of qualification: Certificate, Advanced Certificate and Diploma, the latter qualifying students for membership. Courses are run by the Institute itself and also by organisations such as the National Extension College, which allows you to learn at your own pace with distance-learning.

CAM was set up to administer exams for a number of professional bodies working in the same broad field. The General Certificate can be taken by students of any of these disciplines but the Diploma is specific to individual disciplines and is aimed more substantively at managers. The subjects for the Certificate are Marketing, Advertising, Public Relations, Media and Behavioural Studies, and Sales Promotion and Direct Marketing.

The professional qualification for direct marketing is the DMA UK Diploma and candidates for the subject should contact the Institute of Direct Marketing.

Contact the organisations directly for details of entry requirements. Generally, the exams set by professional bodies start at a fairly basic level so candidates with good GCSE/SCE grades should be able to find a place.

Courses

Many business studies courses allow you the option of studying one of these subjects, or all three sometimes. It is always worth trawling through the various directories to find a course that suits your needs exactly. If you want to study a particular subject in depth, the following courses are available at either HND/HNC or degree level.

Advertising and Advertising Design

HND, Falmouth College of Arts, the London Institute, West Herts College, University of Wolverhampton

BA Hons, Bournemouth University, Lancaster University, the London Institute

Communication Studies

HND, Dewsbury

BA Hons, Bangor Normal College, Bournemouth University, Colchester Institute, University of East London, the London Institute, Middlesex University, University of Ulster

Copywriting/Art Direction

HND, Doncaster College, Falmouth College of Arts, Newcastle College, St Helens College, South East Essex College of Arts and Technology, Stockport College of Further and Higher Education, West Thames College

BA Hons, Manchester Metropolitan University

Marketing and Marketing Design

HND, Bolton Institute of Higher Education, Edinburgh's Telford College, Harper Adams Agricultural College, University of Northumbria at Newcastle, West Herts College, Writtle College (rural resource management)

BA Hons, Bournemouth University, Cheltenham and Gloucester College of Higher Education, Farnborough College of Technol-

Marketing, Advertising and Public Relations

ogy, University of Greenwich, University of Huddersfield, University of Humberside, Leeds Metropolitan University, Napier University, University of Newcastle upon Tyne, Southampton Institute, University of Teesside

Public Relations

BA Hons, Bournemouth University, Leeds Metropolitan University, the London Institute, College of St Mark and St John

There are other related course listings in Chapters 2 and 9.

Useful Addresses

Advertising Association, 15 Wilton Road, London SW1V 1LT; 0171 828 4831
Chartered Institute of Marketing (CIM), Moor Hall, Cookham, Maidenhead, Berkshire SL6 9QH; 01628 524922
Institute of Direct Marketing, 1 Park Road, Teddington, Middlesex TW11 0AR; 0181 977 5705
Institute of Practitioners in Advertising (IPA), 44 Belgrave Square, London SW1X 8QR; 0171 235 7020
Institute of Public Relations, 15 Northborough Street, London EC1V 0AH; 0171 253 5151
Institute of Sales and Marketing Management, National Westminster House, 31 Upper George Street, Luton, Bedfordshire LU1 2RD; 01582 411130
Institute of Sales Promotion, Arena House, 66–68 Pentonville Road, London N1 9HS; 0171 837 5340
National Extension College, 18 Brooklands Avenue, Cambridge CB2 2HN; 01223 316644

Further Reading

The following are all Kogan Page publications:

Everything You Need to Know About Marketing, P Forsyth, 1995
How to Get on in Marketing, 2nd edition, N Hart, N Waite, 1994
How to Market Books, 2nd edition, A Baverstock, 1997
How to Improve Your Marketing Copy, I Linton, 1993
Know Your Customers, J Curry, 1992
Marketing Communications, P Smith, 1993
Practical Marketing, D Bangs, 1993

Working in the Media

The New How to Advertise, K Roman and J Mass, 1992
Effective PR Management, 2nd edition, P Winner, 1993
The Essentials of Public Relations, S Black, 1993

Trade Press

Campaign, Marketing, Marketing Week, Media Week, PR Week, UK Press Gazette

Chapter 9

Art and Design and Photography

Introduction

Entering art and design inevitably means spending between two and five years or more in further and higher education. Few people manage to succeed as practising artists or designers without having been through an art or design education.

Courses provide the creative, theoretical, technical and personal elements that combine to equip their graduates with the basic skills and attitudes they need to begin their careers. Often, it is not until near completion of their courses that many people actually become aware of exactly where their true interests and abilities lie.

As there are over 100 different subject titles in art and design, covering six broad topic areas, this may make life difficult for you now. Even if you know what subject area you want to take, and many people won't, choosing the right course from the vast selection on offer isn't always that straightforward.

You could choose a course which combines academic study and practical skills, a course that has little or no academic content, a purely academic course, a course combining subjects within art and design, or a specialist course which concentrates on one particular discipline. Many students start off with a foundation course or a one-year General Art and Design BTEC course before going on to a higher level course. This has the advantage of introducing you to areas not yet explored, as well as enhancing existing skills.

Which Subject?

Fashion and Textile Design

These courses exist at all levels of qualification. There are normally two main areas of study: fashion design – garment and accessory design; and textile design, printed, knitted or woven – for fashion or furnishing and decorative use, ie furnishing fabrics, wall hangings, curtain fabrics, etc. The courses involve creative, academic and technical aspects; for example, professional design practice, weaving, printing and dyeing. Some will even teach fashion promotion, management studies and accounting and a few offer a fashion illustration option for people who would like to work as fashion illustrators. Fashion design students aspire to work in fashion houses creating original lines of clothing, either for a specialist niche or a mass market. Some students leave college to set up their own house but most work as assistants to other designers. An original idea and good business sense make working for yourself a possibility. Textile design suffers from a declining textile industry in Britain but there are still opportunities, either as a freelance designer for some of the large textile companies or a small design workshop, or even as a designer/craftsperson creating work for exhibition, direct sale or through limited retail craft outlets.

Fine Art

Fine art courses are most commonly offered at degree level. They allow students to explore, and hopefully discover, the nature of their talent. Most fine art departments offer painting, sculpture and printmaking (lithography, etching, film, video and photography). Some departments ask you to choose one area to specialise in, while others give you the opportunity to work in all three. You will not receive training as a craftsperson and although you will be taught how to handle tools, creativity and freedom of expression with the materials are the chief aims. There are no recognised vocational ends so most students see the course as an intellectual and creative exercise in its own right. But far from emerging from college as unemployable misfits, fine art graduates enter a wide range of jobs and occupations both related and unrelated to art and design. Art teaching seems an obvious way of maintaining an involvement with work while earning a living, and other graduates work for museums, arts organisations and in design areas like advertising. Some students do set out from college with the aim of developing their work, possibly seeking commissions, selling work to galleries, and arranging individual and group shows of their work.

Graphic Design

This has a number of different disciplines under the one broad heading: design studies, film and animation, typography and lettering, illustration, printing processes and printmaking, display and exhibition work, technical graphics for engineering, calligraphy, model-making, packaging, design for advertising and so on. The design course teaches the basic principles, exploring the elements of visual communication. Some courses also allow you to pursue a specialist subject throughout and modern computer technology, as well as film, television and video, are regular features of most courses. Course work is geared towards projects where students follow a design 'brief' and submit to a deadline.

Graphic design graduates find work in a variety of different areas. Advertising agencies employ good all-rounders who can visualise ideas for packaging, television advertising, point-of-sale display and so on. Design consultancies work on one-off jobs for industrial and commercial companies and usually specialise in one of the following areas: graphic, package, product, display, exhibition, textile, furniture or interior. Book and magazine publishers employ designers as art assistants and art directors to work on the visual appearance of their products. Graphic designers in television work on typography, lettering, credits and captions, mobiles, weather charts, cartoons and animation, props and programming design. Technical graphic artists work for industrial companies, often allied to the engineering or construction industries. The work requires good interpretation skills in converting figures to two- and three-dimensional drawings. Other employers are universities, local authority public relations departments, exhibition organisers and record companies.

Freelance work is possible after only one or two years with an organisation, depending on your interpretative skills, imagination, drive and contacts. Some sectors, like television, only employ freelance designers.

Working in the Media

Illustration

Illustration is a separate area of study within the general graphic design area. Although illustrators may take the same degrees as graphic designers, they are more likely to specialise. After leaving college they may find full-time employment but are more often commissioned freelances working for publishers, design consultancies, advertising agencies and so on. Scientific and technical illustrators often work for medical and scientific publishers, research establishments, government departments, the National Health Service and so on.

Freelance workers usually come from a background of full-time, part-time or temporary work (which gives them a chance to build up contacts) but others may get work before they leave college by attracting the eye of an ad agency art director or artists' agent, either by submitting a portfolio of work while at college, or by displaying work in the final year show. Artists' agents find work for artists but often charge 25 per cent, or more, commission. Some illustrators work in groups and are able to afford rent for a collective studio. Working together as a co-operative is also possible but you would have to decide whether you prefer solitude when you work.

History of Art and Design

This subject allows students who are not necessarily interested in pursuing a creative artistic activity themselves an opportunity to study the appreciation, criticism and history of art. Some art and design courses include art history components which support and complement your creative work, but if you want to become a real expert the chances are you will need to take a BA degree at university. Most courses concentrate on Western European art but some offer more unusual studies of Latin American art, Ancient Greek and Roman art, or the history of film and cinema.

Graduates have a choice of occupations when they leave. Some enter further postgraduate studies which enable them to study a very specialised historical subject. Some train as arts administrators, librarians, secretaries, fine art restorers, teachers and museum and art gallery curators. Others enter professional areas such as publishing as copywriters and researchers, and the rest follow career occupations in industry, commerce and government. Teachers either study for a Bachelor of Education (BEd) which gives them Qualified Teacher Status (QTS) or follow a BA degree with a one-year postgraduate certificate in education (PGCE), which also gives them QTS.

Three-dimensional Design

This is offered at all levels, and at a wide range of colleges. It explores the design of objects within an actual space. The disciplines include: chief studies in furniture design, wood, glass, metal, ceramics, plastics, jewellery, silversmithing and industrial design. Graduates can choose to produce one-off objects in their own workshops or work on designs to be produced on a larger scale by the manufacturing industry. Known as industrial and product design, this last discipline has tremendous scope for a designer who wishes to influence the living environment. They may be employed in design consultancies or with in-house design groups, although some prefer to work freelance and build their own prototypes, with the aim of persuading a manufacturer to produce their designs commercially. The product designer is chiefly concerned with the aesthetic appearance of the product, but may also take into account the users' needs, the manufacturing requirements and the budget.

Interior Design

This is a three-dimensional study which is concerned with the design of living, working and leisure space inside buildings. Courses will include creative, technical and professional design elements and graduates go on to pursue a number of careers, joining design practices, working freelance or becoming a member of a design unit within a particular industrial company.

Theatre Design

Theatre design is a very specialised field within three-dimensional studies and related employment includes TV set design and exhibition design. Students are given design projects and spend time learning the basics of costume-making, set construction, scene painting and so on. Working closely with other members of the theatre production team, the designer creates a set, from sketches and scale models to the full-blown thing, using a unified design theme. An ability to see the whole process through, without going over budget, is essential. College leavers usually start off as assistants with small repertory companies, often in support roles, painting scenery or making costumes. Others may find themselves working for national theatre, opera and dance companies, or in film and television.

Working Out a Path

Which Qualification?

With such a wide range of qualifications available, how do you choose the right course for you? Most people, but not all, take a foundation course, not only because it enables them to get a good grounding in the subject but also because a lot of university and college courses won't except students without it. After that you have to decide between a BTEC Ordinary Diploma and Certificate, a Higher National Diploma and Certificate, a professional qualification, a Diploma in Higher Education, degrees and postgraduate study. The Kogan Page book, *Careers in Art and Design* is useful because it outlines the various components of each qualification and should give you a clearer idea of why one type of course may be more suitable than another. Only degree, DipHE and BTEC Higher Diploma students are guaranteed grant funding. If you wish to know the status of the other courses, you must contact your local education authority. All grant applications should be submitted by the end of March.

Getting Established

Artists and craftspeople may need to find a funding source to get access to a workshop. Government schemes include the Graduate Enterprise Programme, the Business Start-up Scheme and the Crafts Council Setting-up Scheme. There may also be money from the Arts Council, the Prince's Youth Trust, industrial companies, colleges, schools and foundations. Some designers and artists can work from home but many miss the range of facilities found at art college. Regional Arts Boards have addresses of artists and craftspeople, group workshops and studios and shared facilities in your area. The Acme Artists Housing Association and Space both help artists acquire studio premises in London. You might also approach your local council who may have disused property to rent.

Art and Design and Photography

Very few artists and craftspeople are able to make a full-time living, particularly in the early stages. Many continue to supplement their work with full-time or part-time work, or with commercial freelance design work. Establishing outlets for your work can begin at college and many students have already begun freelance work, received commissions and organised exhibitions before leaving. Make as many contacts as possible. They will always be useful.

Art galleries, arts festivals, arts centres and even commercial companies such as banks may be willing to display your work. The Crafts Council maintains a list of craft galleries and shops.

Freelance designers, whether in textiles, graphics, production, or whatever, can publish themselves through advertising in the local press or selected journals, and through entries in directories such as *The Creative Handbook*.

Photography

Photography is an international means of communication, its great advantage over the written word being that it does not need to be translated for use in another country. The uses of photography range from commercial and press to medicine and crime detection. With the advent of microfilming, the storage and retrieval of information have been made much more convenient and involve the use of far less space.

Commercial Photography

This is split into four sectors: advertising, fashion, industrial and general practice. Photographers in advertising and fashion are nearly always freelance, employed for a particular campaign or job. Industrial photographers may be freelance or employed by large organisations where they take photographs for brochures, catalogues, instruction manuals and in-house magazines. General practice photographers are mainly hired to deliver portraiture and wedding photographs.

Photojournalism

Photojournalism and press photographers work for newspapers, magazines, periodicals and technical journals. All these media, particularly the last three, employ freelance as well as in-house staff. Photojournalists are photographers who are able to tell a story with pictures. They are almost always freelance and the main market for their work is magazines. (See Chapter 7 for training details.)

Institutional and Specialist Photography

Scientific photographers are used to provide information essential in a scientific or engineering field. This work may include aerial photography as well as the use of techniques such as holography, photomicrography and macrophotography. The main employers are the Civil Service, private industries and universities. Other institutions that require photographers include museums, trade associations, national parks departments, charities, advisory councils, education authorities and libraries. Photographers are also employed to teach photography in colleges and schools.

There are many ancillary jobs involved in the production of photographs. **Photofinishing laboratories** cater for the enormous amount of amateur films sent in for processing and much of the work is done by machines, which are checked by technicians and quality controllers. Professional laboratories serve the trade and thus allow considerable scope for the craftsperson. Work includes processing, printing, transparency copying, retouching and dye transferring.

The *British Journal of Photography* (BJP) insists that 'it doesn't matter what stage you are at, you can always benefit from a little more training.... As far as your creativity is concerned you only get out what you put in'.

For those starting out there are several routes and a detailed description of what qualifications are required, as well as what courses are available, appear in *Where to Study Photography*, available from the Royal Photographic Society (RPS) for £10.95.

Training

Briefly, photographers can start off taking a job as a studio assistant without any academic qualifications, although GCSEs might be necessary for further studies, and will give you a better chance of getting a job. Most employers will allow their studio assistants to take time off to study for the City & Guilds 7470. If you have got basic academic qualifications and can demonstrate an interest in photography, you could go into a two-year BTEC National Diploma full time or BTEC National Certificate part time. This is a very broad-based photographic education.

A BTEC HND is the next step in vocational education. This two-year course requires more in-depth study, and students generally specialise in one area or another, for example advertising. Most degree courses put more emphasis on theory and academic achievement but there are usually vocational elements.

HND students sometimes have the option of continuing for a third year. This allows them to take a Professional Qualifying Examination, enabling them to use the ABIPP (Associate of the British Institute of Professional Photography) professional acronym. This final year also allows them to reach BA(Hons) status.

There are no formal educational requirements for the photo lab sector, but training is available in HND form. The two-year full-time course is aimed at managers and includes the various components which would enable you to find work in a photo lab. Most people train on the job and NVQs are now available in photographic processing.

There are also special HND courses in Advertising and Illustrative Photography, Audio Visual, Editorial, Fashion, News and Reportage Photography, Underwater Photography and Electronic Imaging (involving the manipulation of images using computer technology).

A huge range of short courses and photography holidays are also available. To find out more about these contact the Royal Photographic Society.

Useful contacts are the British Institute of Professional Photography, the Royal Photographic Society (who publish the *British Journal of Photography*), the Association of Fashion, Advertising and Editorial Photographers Ltd, the Bureau of Freelance Photographers and the National Council for the Training of Journalists.

Working in the Media

Courses

Art and Design

Key to abbreviations:

A & D – Art and Design; C – College; CA – College of Art; CAD – College of Art and Design; CAT – College of Arts and Technology; CHE – College of Higher Education; CT –College of Technology; CTA – College of Technology and Arts; I – Institute; IAD – Institute of Art and Design; IHE – Institute of Higher Education; MC – Metropolitan College; SA – School of Art; SAD – School of Art and Design; TC – Technical College.

BTEC National Diploma in General Art and Design
Barnfield C, Basingstoke TC, Blackburn C, Cambridge Regional College, Cleveland C, Coventry TC, Croydon C, East Surrey C, Eastbourne C, Falmouth C, Gwent Tertiary C, Henley C, Isle C (Wisbeach), Kensington and Chelsea C, Kent IAD, Loughborough CA, Newcastle under Lyme C, Northampton C, Northbrook C, North East Worcestershire C, North Oxfordshire C, North Warwickshire C, Oldham C, Plymouth CAD, Portsmouth University, St Helens C, Salford CT, Somerset CAT, South Devon C, South East Essex C, Southport C, Southwark C, Stamford C, Strode C, Suffolk C, Surrey IAD, Telford CAT, Thurrock C, Tower Hamlets C, West Cumbria C, West Thames C, Yale C (Wrexham).

BTEC Higher National Diploma in Design
Advertising, Doncaster Metropolitan IHE, Hounslow Borough C, Newcastle CAT
Audio-Visual, Northbrook C
Ceramics, Croydon C, Falmouth SAD, Harrow CHE, Staffordshire University, W Glamorgan IHE
Communications, Cleveland CAD, Dewsbury C, Gloucestershire CAT, North East Wales IHE, Northumberland CAT, Norton C, Suffolk C, Wolverhampton University
Crafts, Carmarthenshire CTA, University of Central England in Birmingham, Chelsea SA, Cumbria CAD, University of Derby, Kent IAD, North East Wales IHE
Fashion/Surface Pattern, Dewsbury C
Fashion/Textiles, Northbrook C
Film and Television, Bournemouth and Poole CAD, Gwent CHE

Art and Design and Photography

Industrial Design, Bournemouth and Poole CAD, Carmarthenshire CTA, Chelsea CAD, Colchester I, Southampton IHE
Interior Design, London Guildhall University
Jewellery, Epsom SAD
Packaging, Swindon C
Retail and Exhibition Design, London C of Printing and Distributive Trades, Salford CT
Textiles, Chelsea SA, Cleveland CAD, University of Derby, Huddersfield University, Somerset CAT
Typography, London College of Printing & Distributive Trades

First Degrees in Art and Design
Bath CHE, Bolton IHE, Bradford and Ilkley Community C, Bretton Hall, Buckinghamshire C, Cardiff IHE, Cheltenham and Gloucester CHE, Crewe and Alsagar CHE, Cumbria CAD, Dartington CA, Edinburgh CA, Falmouth SAD, Farnborough CT, Glasgow SA, Gwent CHE, Hertfordshire CAD, Kent IAD, Kidderminster CFE, Liverpool IHE, London C of Fashion, the London Institute, Loughborough CAD, Norfolk IAD, Ravensbourne C of Design and Communication, Rose Burford C, C of St Mark and St John, University C of St Martin Lancaster, Scottish C of Textiles, Southampton IHE, Suffolk C, Surrey IAD, Swansea IHE, West Herts C, West Surrey CAD, Wimbledon SA, Winchester SA

There are also a huge range of related first degrees, details of which appear in the UCAS *Handbook* and *Official Guide*. More information about art and design courses is given in *Design Courses in Britain*. (£11.50) annual.

Photography

Access Courses, South Cheshire College, Lambeth College, Wulfrun College
C & G 7470 Professional Photography, Brunel College of Arts and Technology, City of Liverpool Community College
BTEC ND in Photography, Brunel College of Arts and Technology, City of Liverpool Community College, Cleveland College of Art and Design, De Montfort University Lincoln, West Kent College, West Herts College, Southport College
BTEC HND in Photography (or related), Bolton Institute of Higher Education, Kent Institute of Art and Design, Salisbury College, Sandwell College of Further Education

Working in the Media

British Institute of Professional Photography PQE specialising in Film and Television, Salisbury College
BA Hons (varied), University of Derby, Napier University, University of Sunderland, University of Westminster

Useful Addresses

Arts Council of Great Britain, 14 Great Peter Street, London SW1P 3NQ; 0171 333 0100
Arts Council of Northern Ireland, 181 Stranmillis Road, Belfast BT9 5DU; 01232 381 591
Arts Council of Wales, Holst House, Museum Place, Cardiff CF1 3NX; 01222 394 711
Association of Fashion, Advertising and Editorial Photographers Ltd, 9 Domingo Street, London EC1Y OTA; 0171 608 1441
British Institute of Professional Photography, Fox Talbot House, Amwell End, Ware, Hertfordshire SG12 9HN; 01920 464011
Bureau of Freelance Photographers, Focus House, 497 Green Lanes, London N13 4BP; 0181 882 3315
Chartered Society of Designers, 29 Bedford Square, London WC1B 3EG
Crafts Council, 44a Pentonville Road, London N1 9HF; 0171 278 7700
Design Council, 28 Haymarket, London SW1Y 4SU; 0171 839 8388
Design Council Manchester, 24th Floor, Sunley Building, Piccadilly Plaza, Manchester M1 4BA
Design Council (Scotland), Ca d'Oro Building, 45 Gordon Street, Glasgow G1 3LZ
Design Council (Wales), QED Centre, Main Avenue, Treforest, Pontypridd CF37 5TR
National Council for the Training of Journalists, Latton Bush Centre, Southern Way, Harlow, Essex CM18 7BL; 01279 430009
Scottish Arts Council, 12 Manor Place, Edinburgh EH3 7DD; 0131 226 6051
Royal Photographic Society, The Octagon, Milsom Street, Bath BA1 1DN; 01225 462841

Further Reading

The Art and Design Directory, Mike Stallard, AVEC Designs, annual
Art, Design and Craft – A Manual for Business Success, J Crowe and J Stokes, Hodder, 1988
Art World Directory, Arts Review, annual
Careers in Art and Design, Linda Bell and Noel Chapman, Kogan Page, 1996
The Creative Handbook, Reed Information Services.
Design Courses in Britain, Trotman and Co, annual
Guide to Courses and Careers in Art, Craft and Design, Tony Charlton, National Society for Education in Art and Design.
The Professional Practice of Design, D Goslett, Batsford, 1983
Registration Scheme: Admissions to BA and BTEC Higher Diploma Courses in Art and Design. ADAR (Art and Design Admissions Registry), annual
Where to Study Photography, Edwin Martin, British Journal of Photography, annual

Chapter 10

How to Get a Job in the Media

Education and Training

Introduction

Choosing a career means choosing a lifestyle, a place to work and a way of working. Few people decide at 16 what they will be doing when they are 40 and reach 40 without changing their minds along the way but, everyone at 16, 18 and, if they are a university undergraduate, 21, has to decide the course of their immediate future, especially if they are considering qualifications.

Some jobs, for example newspaper journalism, require entrants to complete a compulsory training programme. Others may also prefer candidates to have some sort of professional training and it is worth writing to one of the professional bodies or trade unions, or to an employer for whom you would like to work, to find out exactly what type of training is required. Before you enrol on a course, make sure that it will lead to a relevant, recognised/accredited qualification. *British Qualifications*, published annually by Kogan Page, has this sort of information.

If you have decided which type of work appeals to you, and have identified a goal to aim for, your next decision will be whether to continue in full-time higher education by going on to take a course at a college, or apply to join a company's training scheme which will give you the qualifications and experience you need.

If you are undecided, it's probably a good idea to continue with full-time education, if possible. Concentrate on subjects that are always marketable (especially maths and sciences) if you know you will be able to do well at them, or on subjects that will allow freedom of choice later. Most occupations allow you to use a general degree like history or English as currency for gaining further qualifications or a place on a company training programme.

Getting a place on a degree course is by no means easy, and disappointing A level results often require students to rethink their strategy. About 40,000 applicants who find themselves in this situation each year use the 'clearing' process, which amounts to a facility for students who want to go to university but didn't match the entry requirements of their first choice. Hobsons publish *Rethink*, a magazine for students considering clearance.

You may consider taking a BTEC HND/HNC course, or entering a recognised training programme. These programmes may be based on full-time, block-release (which means you are employed, but are released for unbroken periods of five or six weeks, or more, in order to study) or sandwich format. Entry requirements to the lower level National Certificate and Diploma courses vary, but are normally four GCSE passes, BTEC First or equivalent, and are considered to be at around A level standard.

Also without A levels, several occupations allow post-16 entry, but you must consider that you will be entering the industry at a low level and must be prepared to work your way up the career ladder, without the advantages a degree qualification allows. In fact, this isn't as bad as it may seem. There may actually be some considerable benefit in getting early years of practical work experience, ahead of your rivals. The recognised industry standard for on-the-job training is the National Vocational Qualification (NVQ) or Scottish Vocational Qualification (SVQ). The five different levels are recognised in Britain, and soon in the EU, as a standard of achievement which employers can rely on.

Some occupations demand degree level qualifications so if you really want to be a broadcast journalist, for example, you will almost certainly need to study for at least four years before you start work.

Degree Courses

Degree courses are classified as either 'vocational', meaning they are relevant to a specific career, 'semi-vocational', which means they may be of some relevance to the job you are after, and 'non-vocational', which assumes you were not considering a particular degree for its merits as a job winner, but for the academic interest which the subject provides. Often known as general degrees, a large number of students carry on studying their favourite school subject at university to take advantage of the wide variety of possible experiences on offer there, and to come out after three or four years with a recognised qualification that will allow them to enter an occupation at a higher level.

As there is such a wide range of university courses it is useful to consider which one will enable you to combine enjoyment of the subject with positive career value. Modularisation has given many students the opportunity to choose a variety of subjects and CAT (Credit Accumulation and Transfer) allows individuals to earn points towards their degree by taking some courses which are not part of a conventional degree structure, thus allowing students to study at their own pace. If you would rather take a correspondence course, the Open University offers a wide range of subjects at degree level.

Applying

The minimum entry requirement for a degree course is three GCSE passes and two A level or H Grade SCE in Scotland. Combinations of AS and A levels, and BTEC National Certificate and Diploma are also acceptable. *University and College Entrance: The Official Guide* from Sheed and Ward Ltd, 14 Coopers Row, London EC3N 2BH, price £12 plus £3 p&p, lists courses and entry requirements. All applications to university courses must be submitted through UCAS (Universities and Colleges Admission Service) so the UCAS *Handbook* is an essential acquisition. Apart from listing all full-time and sandwich courses, it offers guidance through the application procedure.

Applicants using UCAS can apply for six choices of university and college. Make sure your qualifications satisfy the institution's 'matriculation' requirements as well as those required by the course. The best way to check out these requirements is by consulting the university prospectuses themselves. These are free and sent to you on demand. You will have the opportunity to tell the university about yourself in a space provided on the form. It is useful to photocopy this and practise before you fill in the application form for real. Each form must be accompanied by a registration fee, usually payable by cheque to UCAS. At the time of going to press this was £12, or £4 if you are only applying to one institution.

You will need to do all this research a long time before your first term. UCAS acts as an agent between you and the university, sending on copies of your application to each of the universities on your form, who then decide whether to interview you, offer you a place at an open day or reject you. An offer will be unconditional if you already have the necessary qualifications, or more usually, conditional on successfully obtaining these qualifications.

Applications to UCAS can be submitted from September onwards, the year before you wish to start your course. The closing date for Oxford and Cambridge is 15 October and, for all other entries, 15 December. When you have received all your offers you must accept a firm and insurance offer by 15 May. These dates may vary from year to year so confirm them by looking at the UCAS *Handbook*.

If you are applying for an art and design course you do not apply through UCAS. Instead you apply through the Art and Design Admissions Registry (ADAR). There are different application forms and procedures for foundation courses, degree courses and HND courses. The application times are different to UCAS with the procedure starting on the 1 February 1996, for 1996 entry. The closing date is 31 March. Applicants go through various interview procedures until they find a college which will accept them. Any candidates unplaced by 11 July will receive pool vacancies. Write to ADAR for more details. More information about art and design courses is given in *Design Courses in Britain*, published by Trotman and Co, 12 Hill Rise, Richmond, Surrey, TW10 6UA (£11.50) and in the UCAS *Handbook*.

Choosing the Right Degree Course

Choosing which courses and universities to apply for entails quite a bit of research into your own abilities. There is no point in aiming for a university whose entry requirements are beyond you, so you should discuss your capabilities with your teachers. They will be able to assess more accurately what grades you are likely to achieve.

It is then important to look in great detail at the course content, because it might not offer you what you really want. Although it is very difficult to check the quality of the course, there are certain guidelines to follow. Departments are normally given a research rating which determines the levels of funding they receive for their work. Some university departments have a five-star rating and employ correspondingly good lecturers and tutors. Others will have a good reputation among employers and it might be worth contacting a few major employers to find out what sort of graduate they are looking for. It might not actually make that much difference to them which university course you took. They may be more interested in what you achieved while you were at university, not just academically, but socially. Employers like to see participation in university activities more than just academic brilliance on its own.

Although it is not always a trustworthy record of an establishment's quality, you could always check out the annual league tables to get a general idea of the positioning of your chosen university. Talking to current students will help you once you've got to open days but remember that the students showing you round on the guided tour are usually going to be quite positive about the course anyway. Often, student unions publish alternative prospectuses which give you a much better indication of the quality of student life. Ask to see one when you go for your interview.

You may consider taking a 'sandwich' course where an academic programme is combined with time spent working on the job. This sort of course will be particularly useful for candidates considering a business-related qualification, such as marketing. A 'thick' sandwich course divides the learning programme into three parts – two years in university, one year out, another year in. A 'thin' sandwich divides the first three years between college and employer in equal periods, with the final year spent in college.

As you are spending three or four years at a university it is necessary to consider what non-academic experience you hope to get out of it. Study the facilities within the university and surrounding area. If you want to work in broadcasting, a university with a radio station would be an obvious choice. All student unions offer club facilities, some of which may be useful for your chosen career, for example the film club. Many careers have started in student unions so consider carefully the range of facilities each university offers. Also consider how likely you are to be able to participate in the facilities when you arrive. Although Oxford has a good reputation for its student publications, it may be harder to get involved in activities if you don't already have a high level of writing experience and skill.

Accommodation should also be taken into account. Find out what is on offer from the university and how much private accommodation exists in the area. Some places only offer shared rooms in halls of residences, an experience which can be a nightmare if you end up sharing with someone who goes to bed five hours after you do.

Once you have thought about all these points you may need to research courses further. Read *Which Degree?* (Hobsons), the *Compendium of Advanced Courses in Colleges of Further and Higher Education* and the *Directory of UK Higher Education*, all available at the reference library. You can also look up ECCTIS, a computerised information service covering over 100,000 course opportunities. This can be accessed through your careers office and possibly through your school or college.

Other Courses

As well as degree courses, universities and colleges of higher education provide training for a number of other qualifications. They include foundation courses and professional courses which lead to recognised professional status.

Application for **teacher training** courses, including Art Teacher's Certificate/Diploma courses, is through the UCAS scheme. The NATFHE *Handbook of Initial Teacher Training* lists courses of teaching at both undergraduate and postgraduate levels, including details of courses that normally lead to a Qualified Teacher Status (QTS) award. Costing £12, it is available from Linneys ESL, Newgate Lane, Mansfield, Notts NG18 2PA.

The Royal Society of Arts (RSA) awards qualifications in office skills, including wordprocessing (now essential in many types of career), typing, accounting, computing, information technology and business studies, all of which can be useful in the media. The courses are taken in schools, colleges, training centres and at evening classes.

Some of the courses listed in the following pages are based around home study. **Pitman Training Ltd** offers students a range of 40 different courses using audio-visual and multimedia techniques, starting on any working day. As well as a range of short courses, including shorthand, Pitman runs a Diploma Programme aimed at those wishing to develop a range of office skills. For further details contact Pitman Training Limited, 154 Southampton Row, London WC1B 5AX.

Funding for Education

Awards for Degree Level Courses

These are mandatory, which means that local education authorities are obliged to support students who fulfil the necessary criteria. Courses accepted by the Department for Education and Employment (DfEE) as equivalent to degree courses include BTEC and SCOTVEC Higher National Diplomas, PGCE teacher training courses and DipHe courses.

A full award is supposed to, but very rarely does, cover tuition fees, college dues, student union fees and most of your living expenses, such as accommodation, books, equipment and travel. You are expected to find the rest of the money yourself by taking out a student loan (details of which follow shortly). The grant is means-tested so the amount of grant you get depends on your parents' income. Contributions range from £45 for an income of £15,510 to £5,800 for an income of £60,599. Any shortfall is the responsibility of your parents. The basic grant rates are £2,340 if you are studying in London and £1885 if you are studying elsewhere. Students living with their parents receive a standard grant of £1,530.

You should be able to get the appropriate forms from your school or college, or direct from your LEA in England and Wales; the Student Awards Agency for Scotland; or your local education and library board in Northern Ireland. There are two stages of the application procedure. You send an initial application form and a grant assessment form to the LEA for processing, as soon as you decide which kind of course you want to apply for; and you send a college acceptance form to the college, either when you receive an unconditional offer or later when you know your examination results. This is subsequently passed on by them to your LEA.

Some students have had difficulty when applying because their parents refuse to give details of their income or because they are unable, or unwilling, to pay their parental contribution. When the application form is not completed in full, LEAs will only pay tuition fees, with no contribution towards maintenance. Unfortunately there is no scheme to help students whose parents do not support them but your school or college tutor may be willing to discuss the problem with your parents.

Discretionary grants may be awarded for courses below degree level but there are no national scales or regulations. Write to your LEA for details.

The Student Loan Scheme

This scheme is designed to top-up student grants and any student aged under 50 is eligible. Administered by the Student Loans Company, they are not means-tested and students only start paying back the loan when they start earning a good income (more than 85 per cent of average earnings). The 1996 threshold for paying back the loan was £1,267 per month so any graduates earning less than this in 1996 didn't have to start paying off their debt. The maximum loan available was £1,695 and the minimum £780, depending on whether students live in London, or at home.

Even with a government-backed loan, most students leave university with a bank overdraft and a credit card bill. Earning money during the summer is sometimes the only way students survive during the rest of the year and many take part-time jobs during term time.

Sources of Further Information

Other types of financial help may be available as follows:

Career development loans, a scheme administered by the DfEE in partnership with several national banks (contact 0800 585505).

Sponsorship schemes offered by employers and professional bodies – consult Student Sponsorship Information Service's free leaflet *A Question of Sponsorship*, COIC's (Careers and Occupational Information Centre's) annual publication *Sponsorships*, and *The Which? Guide to Sponsorship in Higher Education*, published by the Consumers' Association and Hodder Headline (0171 873 6000).

Educational trust funds and charities – refer to *The Charities Digest* published by the Family Welfare Association (tel: 0171 254 6251) and the *Directory of Grant-Making Trusts* published by the Charities Aid Foundation (tel: 01732 771333).

Access funds and hardship grants are also administered by individual colleges.

Full details about grants and loans are given in the DfEE leaflet *Student Grants and Loans, A Brief Guide*, available free from the DfEE Publications Centre or from most job centres and career libraries. *Student Grants in Scotland* is published by the Student Awards Agency for Scotland and *Grants and Loans to Students* by the Department of Education for Northern Ireland. In addition, the Welsh Office Education Department publishes a Welsh language booklet on student grants and loans (FHE1 Division, 3rd Floor, Cathays Park, Cardiff CF1 3NQ).

Vocational Training Programmes

Often training is given on the job. This means an employer takes on a suitably qualified applicant with a keen interest in a particular subject and trains him or her to an industry-recognised standard of achievement; increasingly this comes in the form of an NVQ. These schemes allow the trainee to progress on to better paid jobs which demand a higher level of skill and quite often a greater undertaking of responsibility. Some of these training schemes are mentioned in other chapters.

Training For Work

This is intended for people who have been unemployed for over 12 months so they can improve their work-related skills. Training and initial advice is provided by the local Training and Enterprise Council (TEC) or Local Enterprise Council (LEC) in Scotland.

Modern Apprenticeships

These are designed for those aged between 16 and 17. They offer an apprentice training to at least NVQ level 3, which is roughly equivalent to two A levels or an Advanced GNVQ, and a small wage. Each apprenticeship lasts for about three years and the apprentice follows an agreed training plan.

Accelerated Modern Apprenticeships

These offer a similar sort of programme to 18- and 19-year olds.

This time the training lasts no longer than two years.

Youth credits allow you to buy training. They are given to anyone who leaves college at 16 or 17, and their value can range from £750 to well over £5,000, according to your particular needs and the occupational sector you choose. The scheme will vary from area to area so it's worth contacting your local careers advisor to find out what is available in your area. Once you have been given credit you can go and spend it on the training you want, including a modern apprenticeship or one of the wide range of work-based training schemes available through TECs and LECs.

How to Get a Job

Pre-work Preparation

Every employer will be looking for someone who can show some positive evidence of being interested in a particular subject. Although television addiction may be a useful 'asset' if you wish to become the next Noel Edmunds, employers will be more impressed if you turn out to be Mr Blobby. In other words, if you can demonstrate a commitment to a particular occupation by showing you have gained some sort of personal experience as a volunteer or through a work placement programme, you will have a better chance of getting the job you want.

Covering Letters

Most job advertisements will ask you to send a covering letter. This is, as it sounds, a letter to tell the prospective employer that you are enclosing a CV or application form, in answer to so-and-so job advert. However, there is usually (but not always) a hidden agenda with a request for a covering letter. For a covering letter is quite often a cunning plan by the recruiter to see if there are any applications that immediately stand out, and conversely if there are some which can be thrown on the reject pile, thus saving the recruiter the bother of reading through them. Any covering letters which are messy, full of spelling errors, too informal or rude will result in the rest of your brilliantly conceived application package heading straight for the bin. Covering letters are a great opportunity to 'set out your stall'; in other words, tell the employer, briefly, why you will be perfect for the job. Don't ever write, 'I will be perfect for the job because...'. Potential employers may like confidence but they also like originality. Writing about one or two of the achievements mentioned in your CV is often a good way of doing this. As a covering letter is the first thing a recruiter sees, it's worth spending time on this part of your application.

Curriculum Vitae

First impressions last, or so the saying goes. Be sure that a well-presented, concise and informative CV will stand out in any pile of dreary applications. Tactics to get noticed include coloured paper, CVs that are desk-top published and photographs (essential in the acting profession). Always make your CV appropriate for the job you are applying for. A standard CV is OK but material that is written with a particular reader in mind will help your cause no end. Getting advice is always a good idea. *Preparing Your Own CV,* by Rebecca Corfield, is published by Kogan Page. If you can afford it you may wish to buy in the services of a professional CV designer or typist. The Yellow Pages usually has a list.

If you are preparing your own CV, always type it, and make sure there are no errors (especially typing errors). A CV should include:

- Full name and address.
- Date of birth.
- Schools attended.
- Examinations passed (dates and grades).
- Any other honours won at school or college.
- Any particular position of authority held at school.
- Training courses/colleges attended and qualifications gained (dates and grades).
- Previous jobs held or any other experience (names of employers and dates).
- Names and addresses of two referees. One of these should be a previous employer or someone who has personal knowledge of your abilities.
- Personal interests and hobbies, especially those relevant to the job you would like.
- Foreign languages – indicate your level of competence.
- Driving licence. A clean driving licence is needed for many jobs; if you have one, mention it.

Interviews – Portraying the Right Image

You may feel very nervous at an interview and find it difficult to collect your thoughts when asked even quite simple and obvious questions. Interview panels understand nerves and are very forgiving. Even so, most people in interviews can't think of perfect answers to on-the-spot questions so it is a good idea to prepare a few questions and answers in advance. Some of the more commonly asked questions are:

> Why do you want a career in journalism/advertising/publishing (or whatever the area is)?
> What made you apply for this particular job/write to this organisation?
> Why do you think you will be good at this job/you have something to offer this organisation?
> What attracts you to this job/organisation?
> How would you like your career to develop/What would you like to be doing in five/ten years' time?
> (If you already have a job) Why do you want to leave your present job?

Remember that you will be competing for work in an area where flair and proven commitment count for more than qualifications. A degree or recognised diploma will open a few doors, but in the eyes of a potential employer they may well count for less than a portfolio of your published articles, drawings, design work or photographs, a film script or film/video footage, or a demo tape. When you go to an interview you should be able to convince your prospective employer that you have a deep fascination for, say, advertising, or publishing, or whatever occupation you are interested in. You must be able to show that this fascination has driven you to do some work experience or voluntary work already and that the job you are applying for is a continuation of a process already started.

Where to Get Information, Advice and Support

Each occupation has its own sources of information and help, as presented at the end of each chapter. More generally, there are a number of other useful sources of information. These include your local careers advisor, job centres, careers advisory officers and schools liaison officers attached to large companies, and even private companies who offer independent vocational guidance. The UCAS *Official Guide* has a very good list of relevant publications which is updated every year.

General Addresses

Art and Design Admissions Registry (ADAR), Penn House, 9 Broad Street, Hereford HR4 9AP; 01432 266653

Business and Technology Education Council (BTEC) Information Services, Central House, Upper Woburn Place, London WC1H 0HH; 0171 413 8405/6

Central Bureau for Educational Visits and Exchanges, 10 Spring Gardens, London, SW1A 2BN; 0171 389 4426

City & Guilds of London Institute (C&G), 1 Giltspur Street, London, EC1A 9DD; 0171 294 2468

COIC, Moorfoot, Sheffield S1 4PQ; 0114 259 4563/4/9

Department for Education and Employment (DfEE), Sanctuary Building, Great Smith Street, London SW1P 3BT; 0171 925 5000

Department of Education, Northern Ireland, Rathgael House, Balloo Road, Bangor, County Down BT19 7PR; 01247 279279

ECCTIS 2000, Fulton House, Jessop Avenue, Cheltenham, Gloucestershire GL50 3SH; 01242 518724

Educational Grants Advisory Service, c/o Family Welfare Association, 501-505 Kingsland Road, Dalston, London E8 4AU; 0171 254 6251

National Council for Vocational Qualifications (NCVQ), 222 Euston Road, London NW1 2BZ; 0171 387 9898

National Extension College, 18 Brooklands Avenue, Cambridge CB2 2HN; 01223 316644

Open University, Central Enquiry Service, PO Box 200, Wilton Hall, Milton Keynes, Buckinghamshire MK7 6YZ; 01908 653231

RSA Examinations Board, Westwood Way, Coventry CV4 8HS; 01203 470033

Scottish Office Education Department, Student Awards, Gyleview House, 3 Redheughs Rigg, South Gyle, Edinburgh EH12 9HH; 0131 244 5823

Scottish Vocational Education Council (SCOTVEC), Hanover House, 24 Douglas Street, Glasgow G2 7NQ; 0141 248 7900

Skill: National Bureau for Students with Disabilities, 336 Brixton Road, London SW9 7AA; 0171 274 0565

Student Loans Company, 100 Bothwell Street, Glasgow G2 7JD; 01345 300900

UK ERASMUS Student Grants Council, The University, Canterbury, Kent CT2 7PD; 01227 762712

Universities and Colleges Admissions Service (UCAS), Fulton House, Jessop Avenue, Cheltenham, Gloucestershire GL50 3SH; 01242 227788

Index

account manager 98
accountant 11
acquisitions editor 63
actor 43–5
advertisement sales 67
advertising 98
   courses 104–5
   degree courses 102
   getting started 100–102
   qualifications 102
advertising agency 96, 98
agency producer 99
agents 44, 56–8
airtime sales staff 11–12
announcer 12
apprenticeship 128–9
art and design 107
   career path 112
   courses 115–17
   first degrees 117
   getting established 112–13
   history of 110–11
   qualifications 112
art director 98
art editor 66
artist 68
arts administration
   administrator 53
   courses 58
   degree level qualifications 59
   job opportunities 52–4
arts administrators
   entry requirements 54–5
   personal qualities 54–5
   training 54–5
Arts Council 44, 75
ASM (assistant stage manager) 39
assistant director, film/video 27

Association of Independent Radio Companies (AIRC) 22

BBC 2, 7–8, 34–5, 87
BECTU 1, 25, 31
BFI Film and Television Handbook 22
binding and finishing 70
book club editor 64
book publishing 60–61
   electronic media 62
   job opportunities 62–4
bookbinder 70
box office staff 41
British Film Institute (BFI) 1, 22, 75
British Sky Broadcasting (BSkyB) 9
broadcasting 7–23
   courses and trainingschemes 22–3
   employers 7–11
   getting started 21–2
   job opportunities 11–20
   journalism 87–8
   writing 78
   see also radio; television
BTEC HND 13, 115
BTEC HND in Design 116
BTEC HND/HNC 121
BTEC National Certificate 115
BTEC National Diploma in General Art and Design 116
BTEC/SCOTVEC Higher National Certificate and Diploma 103
BTEC/SCOTVEC qualifications 59
busking 49

Index

Cable TV 9
camera operator 12, 27, 69
casting director 12, 39
CD-ROM 62
Ceefax 8
Central Bureau for Educational Visits and Exchanges 6
Channel Four 1, 9, 35
children's books 78
choreographer 46
cinematographer 27
circulation 67
Classic FM 3, 10
commissioning editor 63
community radio 11, 22
computer technology 1, 2
concert agent 58
concerts manager 53
continuity person 12
continuity personnel 26
co-operative ventures 1
copy-editor 68
copyright editor 64
copywriter 98
costume design 12–13
CSV media 33
Curriculum Vitae (CV) 130
Cyfle 34

dance animateur 46
dancer 45–6
degree courses 121–5
  awards 126
design, *see* art and design; graphic design
designer
  publishing 65, 66
  theatre 39
desk editor 63
director
  film/video 26
  theatre 39
director of photography 27
DJ, *see* presenter
drama
  courses 43
  therapy 49
  see also theatre

dresser 13
dressmaker 13

editor 62, 66
  broadcasting 13–14
  film 28
editorial assistant 63–4, 66
editorial director 62–3
editorial services 67
education and training 120–29
  funding 126–7
electronic news gathering (ENG) editors 14
EMAP 4
entertainment industry 46
Equity 46–7
European Economic Area 6
European Media School 33
European Union (EU) 5–6

fashion design 108
feature films 78
festival director 53
festivals 49, 53, 55
fiction 77
Film and Television Freelance Training (FT2) 30
film industry 24–37
  courses 31–2
  degree level qualifications 32–3
  education and training 30–31
  further reading 37
  getting started 28–30
  job opportunities 24–5
  training schemes 33–4
  useful addresses 34–6
film librarian 14
film-making process 25–8
film school 31
financial help 127–8
fine art 108–9
floor manager (broadcasting) 14
freelances 4–5, 46, 67–8, 74, 89, 110

Gaelic Television Training Trust 34
global publishing 2

Government Press Service (GPS) 88–9
graphic design 14, 109

health warning 21
history of art and design 110–11
house manager 41

illustration 110
Independent Local Radio (ILR) 10–11
Independent National Radio 35–6
Independent Television Network (ITV) 3, 7–11
Independent Television News (ITN) 9
independent television production companies 10
indexing 68
information sources 131–2
information superhighway 2
Institute of Practitioners in Advertising (IPA) 101
Institute of Public Relations 101
interactive multimedia packages 2
interior design 111
Internet 2
interviews 131

job advertisements 129
job applications 129–32
job opportunities 4–5
job vacancies, EU 6
journalism 15, 82–94
   broadcasting 87–8
   courses 89–92
   getting started 84–5
   qualifications 85
   training 83–4, 86

language skills 6
lexicography 68
lighting director 15
lighting electrician 15
lighting engineer 41
literary agent 57
literary services 67

Local Enterprise Council (LEC) 128
local radio stations 22
location manager 15

machine minder 69
magazines 66, 67, 76–7, 85–6
make-up artist 15–16, 40–41
managing director 53
market research 96
marketing 65–6, 96–7
   courses 104–5
   degree courses 102
   getting started 100–102
   qualifications 102
marketing manager 96
Media Courses UK 22
media industry 1–4
media planner 99
Murdoch, Rupert 2
music agent 58
music therapy 49
musician 46

National Council for Drama Training (NCDT) 43
National Council for the Training of Broadcast Journalists (NCTBJ) 87
National Council for the Training of Journalists (NCTJ) 83
National Film and Television School 31
National Lottery 54
National Vocational Qualifications (NVQ) 22, 71, 83, 128
newspapers 76–7, 82–3
newsroom staff 15
non-fiction 77

operational engineer 16
overseas employment 5–6

paperback editor 64
partnerships 1
performer 16, 42–3
   courses 50
periodical publishing 66

Index

permissions editor 64
personnel manager 53
photography 113–15
   commercial 113
   courses 117–18
   institutional 114
   scientific 114
   specialist 114
   training 114–15
photojournalism 113–14
picture researcher 64
Pitman Training Ltd 125
planner/platemaker 69
presenter 13, 16
press agency 88
press officer 42, 89
press photography 83, 113–14
pre-work preparation 129
printing
   courses 72
   job opportunities 69–70
   qualifications and training 70–71
producer
   broadcasting 16
   film/video 26
   theatre 38
Production and Casting Report (PCR) 44
production assistant (PA), broadcasting 16–17
production controller, publishing 65
production director, publishing 65
production electrician 15
production manager, film/video 26
production services 67
production staff
   publishing 66–7
   theatre 40
programme assistant 17
programme director 17
promoter 53
proofreader 68, 69
property staff 17, 40
public relations 89, 97, 99–100
   courses 104–5
   degree courses 102
   getting started 100–102
   qualifications 102
publicist 67
publicity 65–6
publishing 60–68
   allied occupations and freelance opportunities 67–8
   courses 71–2
   specialist 61–2
   see also book publishing

qualifications 6

RADA 44
radio 3
   independent 10
   journalism 87
   see also broadcasting
reader 68
receptionist 29
researcher 17–18
Royal Society of Arts (RSA) 125
runner (or messenger) 29

sales 65–6
sales team 96
Scottish Broadcast and Film Training Ltd 33
script editor 18
secretarial positions 18
secretary 29
Services Sound and Vision Corporation (SSVC) 11
set designer 18
short-term contract 5
Single Market 6
Skillset 22, 87
SOCRATES programme 6
sound engineer 41
sound mixer 18, 27
sound operator 18–19
sound recordist 27
specialist engineer 19
sponsoring editor 63
sponsorship 55–6
   entry requirements 56
   personal qualities 56
   training 56

Working in the Media

Spotlight 44
Stage, The 44
stage crew 40
stage manager 19, 39
stagehands 19
student loan scheme 127
studio floor manager 28
sub-editor 66

Teletext 10
television 3
   journalism 87
   see also broadcasting
textile design 108
theatre 38–51
   alternative 48
   backstage 38–42
   children's 48
   community 48
   courses 50
   work scene 46–7
   working in London 47
   working in the regions 47–8
theatre design 111–12
theatre manager 52
theatrical agent 57–8
three-dimensional design 111
trade unions 1, 2
trainee engineer 19
Training and Enterprise Council (TEC) 128
training for work 128
translation 68, 78–9

transmission controller 19–20

UK ERASMUS 6

video industry 24–37
   courses 31–2
   degree level qualifications 32–3
   education and training 30–31
   further reading 37
   getting started 28–30
   job opportunities 24–5
   training schemes 33–4
   useful addresses 34–6
videotape librarian 14
Virgin Radio 10
vision mixer 20
visual effects designer 20
vocational training programmes 128

wardrobe work 40–41
weather forecasts 20
Welsh Fourth Channel (S4C) 9
women's training organisations 34
writing 74–81
   courses 80
   getting started 79–80
   job opportunities 74–80
   markets 75–80
   training 80
writing for broadcasting 20

Yellow Pages 22, 24, 101

Suggested Further Reading

The Kogan Page Careers in... Series:

Accountancy *(6th edition)*
Architecture *(4th edition)*
Art and Design *(7th edition)*
Banking and Finance
   (4th edition)
Environmental Conservation
   (6th edition)
Film and Video *(5th edition)*
Journalism *(7th edition)*
The Law *(7th edition)*
Marketing, Advertising and
   Public Relations *(6th edition)*
Medicine, Dentistry and Mental
   Health *(7th edition)*
Nursing and Related Professions
   (7th edition)
Police Force *(4th edition)*
Publishing and Bookselling
   (2nd edition)
Retailing *(5th edition)*
Secretarial and Office Work
   (7th edition)
Social Work *(6th edition)*
Sport *(6th edition)*
Teaching *(6th edition)*
Television and Radio *(6th edition)*
The Theatre *(5th edition)*
Travel Industry *(5th edition)*
Using Languages *(7th edition)*
Working Outdoors *(6th edition)*
Working with Animals
   (7th edition)
Working with Children and Young
   People *(6th edition)*

Also Available from Kogan Page:

Creating Your Career, Simon Kent
Great Answers to Tough Interview Questions: How to Get the Job You Want (3rd edition), Martin John Yate
How to Pass Graduate Recruitment Tests, Mike Bryon
How to Pass Numeracy Tests, Harry Tolley and Ken Thomas
How to Pass Selection Tests, Mike Bryon and Sanjay Modha
How to Pass Technical Selection Tests, Mike Bryon and Sanjay Modha
How to Pass the Civil Service Qualifying Tests, Mike Bryon
How to Pass Verbal Reasoning Tests, Harry Tolley and Ken Thomas
How You Can Get That Job!: Application Forms and Letters Made Easy, Rebecca Corfield
How to Win as a Part-Time Student, Tom Bourner and Phil Race
Job Hunting Made Easy (3rd edition), John Bramham and David Cox
The Kogan Page Guide to Working in Arts, Crafts and Design (2nd edition), David Shacklady (ed.)
Manage Your Own Career, Ben Bell
Preparing Your Own CV, Rebecca Corfield
Readymade Job Search Letters, Lynn Williams
Test Your Own Aptitude (2nd edition), Jim Barrett and Geoff Williams
Your First Job (3rd edition), Vivien Donald and Ray Grose